W9-AYY-750

# A New Method
## *To Speak, Read andWrite*
# Arabic

# العربيــة

للناطقين باللّغة الإنجليزية

# A New Method

## *To Speak, Read and Write*

# Arabic

المؤلـــف

**عبد الرحمن علوش**

**دار الشمال**

**للطباعة والنشر والتوزيع**

# DAR EL-CHIMAL

**PRINTING - PUBLISHING**
**DISTRIBUTING**



TRIPOLI - LIBAN - P.B.: 57 - Fax: 00961 6 442485
Tall - Centre Arja - Tél/Fax: 00961 6 431952
Maarad - Imm. La Cité - Tél/Fax: 00961 6 442489
Sagha - Tél/Fax: 00961 6 438560
E-mail: elchimal@inco.com.lb





1st Edition

2001

# Preface

The Arabic language is not easy to learn. It needs effort and perseverance. But as soon as the student acquires the necessary and fundamental knowledge of it , he will be interested.

I have had much experience in teaching both languages to students in different classes up to the high school certificate.

During this experience, I developed an idea about the student's need to learn how to speak, read and write Arabic.

Arabic grammar is very wide and has many exceptions and subrules. I dealt with only the necessary topics for the beginner in the simplest and easiest method.

This book contains vocabulary, topics and exercises, which will help the foreign student in his daily life while being in contact. with the Arabs. It also contains recorded exercises to practice speaking Arabic correctly.

I have thought it would be useful to add some well - chosen Arabic proverbs and their counterparts in English.

In the end, I don't assume that this work is perfect. I did my best to make it as a guide to help the English student who wishes to learn Arabic. I hope it fulfils the aim beyond it, and I will be thankful for any positive and fruitful criticism.

The Arabic language was always an important language of culture in the medieval times. It spread through many countries in the East and in the West. Nowadays, it is one of the International languages, and more than two hundred million people speak and write Arabic. It is useful for the foreigner to learn this language, to become acquainted with the culture and tradition of the Arab people whose country is rich with natural resources and beautiful scenery.

***Abdul Rahman Alloush***

# 1 Arabic Alphabets - Conventions الحـــروف العـــربيـــة

أشكالها وما يقابلها بالانجليزية

Dear student! We are glad to know that you are interested to learn Arabic. Learning this language will be helpful when you think to visit the Arab countries for business, pleasure, or other purposes.

Learning a foreign language needs patience, perseverance and practice. The Arabic language is different from European languages in two aspects:

a - The words of this language are formed of connected alphabets.

b - The words have vowel signs on them, and some have dots.

After this short and necessary introduction, let us proceed to introduce you - my dear student - to the Arabic Alphabets. Arabic Alphabets are twenty eight in number having two more alphabets than the English language. These alphabets have more than one shape according to their position in the word. Here are these alphabets:

| | | | | | |
|---|---|---|---|---|---|
| (as in tea) | t = ت | (as in boy) | b = ب | (as in ant) | a = ا |
| | ḥ = ح | (as in joy) | j = ج | (as in health) | th = ث |
| (as in then) | dh = ذ | (as in day) | d = د | | kh = خ |
| (as in soon) | s = س | (as in zinc) | z = ز | (as in red) | r = ر |
| | ḍ = ض | (as in son) | ṣ = ص | (as in shine) | sh = ش |
| | ʿa = ع | | ḍh = ظ | (as in but) | ṭ = ط |
| | q = ق | (as in foot) | f = ف | | gh = غ |
| (as in moon) | m = م | (as in late) | L = ل | (as in keen) | k = ك |
| (as in wet) | w = و | (as in hot) | h = هـ | (as in not) | n = ن |
| | | | | (as in yes) | y = ي |

**Notes:** 1 - The Arabic letter is «w» at the beginning, but «u» in the middle of the word (as in university).

2 - The Arabic letter «ي» is «y» at the beginning, but «i» in the middle of the word.

3 - The English letters = V, P, G, have no similar letters in Classical Arabic.

4 - Some letters have a little different shape according to their position in the sentence. Here are some of them:

| | | | |
|---|---|---|---|
| ب b = بـ، ـبـ | ت t = تـ، ـتـ | ث th = ثـ، ـثـ | ج j = جـ، ـجـ |
| ح ḥ = حـ، ـحـ | خ kh = خـ، ـخـ | س s = سـ، ـسـ | ش sh = شـ، ـشـ |
| ص ṣ = صـ | ض ḍ = ضـ | ع ȃ = عـ، ـعـ | غ gh = غـ، ـغـ |
| ف f = فـ | ق q = قـ | ك k = كـ، ـك | م m = مـ |
| ن n = نـ | هـ h = ـهـ، ـه، ه | ي y = يـ، ـيـ | |

## Recorded Exercise 1 — تمريـن مسجّل 1

I pronounce the Following letters:

ب ب ب – ت ت ت – ث ث ث – ج ج ج – د د د – ذ ذ ذ – ر ر ر – ز ز ز –
س س س – ش ش ش – ف ف ف – ك ك ك – ل ل ل – م م م – ن ن ن

## Recorded Exercise 2 — تمريـن مسجّل 2

I pronounce the Following letters:

ا ا ا – ح ح ح – خ خ خ – ص ص ص – ض ض ض – ط ط ط – ظ ظ ظ –
ع ع ع – غ غ غ – ق ق ق – هـ هـ هـ – و و و – ي ي ي

## 2 Vowel Sounds

## الحركاتُ العربَيّة 2

The Arabic Alphabets have three vowel sounds as:

e = ـــِـ والكَسْرَة o = ـــُـ الضَمَّة a = ـــَـ الفَتْحَة

The long vowel sounds are

«a» for the Arabic letter «ا»,

«u» for the Arabic letter «و»,

and «i» for the Arabic letter «يـ» in the middle of the word.

We have the Arabic letter called «hamzeh " ء "» which may be above the Arabic letters " ا ", " و ", " ي " or alone on the line.

This is represented by ـؐـ above the letter. We have also the repeated letter called «Shaddeh» in Arabic.

This is represented by putting this sign « ّ » above the letter as«دّ», «صّ»,

**N.B.** 1 - If the Arabic letter is silent, has no vowel sound on it, this letter will have a small circle on it. This small circle is called sokun in Arabic. "ـْـ"

It is represented by "o" on the letter.

2- This sign "-" on the letter means that we have to open our mouth wide up when we utter this letter.

## Recorded Exercise 3 — تمريـن مسجّل 3

I read: (Alphabets with different vowel sounds) ảqraả :أَقْرَأُ

| | | | |
|---|---|---|---|
| ba = بَ | ta = تَ | ja = جَ | tha = ثَ |
| bo = بُ | to = تُ | jo = جُ | tho = ثُ |
| be = بِ | te = تِ | je = جِ | the = ثِ |
| fa = فَ | ma = مَ | ka = كَ، کَ | la = لَ |
| fo = فُ | mo = مُ | ko = كُ، کُ | lo = لُ |
| fe = فِ | me = مِ | ke = كِ، کِ | le = لِ |
| na = نَ | ḥa = حَ | da = دَ | ra = رَ |
| no = نُ | ḥo = حُ | do = دُ | ro = رُ |
| ne = نِ | ḥe = حِ | de = دِ | re = رِ |
| sa = سَ | ṣa = صَ | za = زَ | qa = قَ |
| so = سُ | ṣo = صُ | zo = زُ | qo = قُ |
| se = سِ | ṣe = صِ | ze = زِ | qe = قِ |

## Recorded Exercise 4 — تمريـن مسجّل 4

I read: (Alphabets: silent and with different vowel sounds) ʾaqraʾa :أَقْرَأُ

| | | | |
|---|---|---|---|
| sha = شَ | ha = هَ، هـَ | wa = وَ | ya = يـَ، يَ |
| sho = شُ | ho = هُ، هـُ | wo = وُ | yo = يـُ، يُ |
| she = شِ | he = هِ، هـِ | we = وِ | ye = يـِ، يِ |
| kha = خَ | ʾaa = ـعَـ، عَ | gha = ـغَـ، غَ | ḍh a = ظَ |
| kho = خُ | ʾao = ـعُـ، عُ | gho = ـغُـ، غُ | ḍh o = ظُ |
| khe = خِ | ʾae = ـعِـ، عِ | ghe = ـغِـ، غِ | ḍhe = ظِ |
| dha = ذَ | ḍa = ضَ | ṭa = طَ | |
| dho = ذُ | ḍo = ضُ | ṭo = طُ | |
| dhe = ذِ | ḍe = ضِ | ṭe = طِ | |
| b = بْ | t = تْ | th = ثْ | j = جْ |
| f = فْ | m = مْ | k = كـْ، كْ | l = لْ |
| n = نْ | ḥ = حْ | d = دْ | r = رْ |
| s = سْ | ṣ = صْ | z = زْ | q = قْ |
| sh = شْ | h = هْ، هـْ | w = وْ | y = يْ |
| kh = خْ | ʾa = ـعْـ، عْ | gh = غْ | ḍh = ظْ |
| dh = ذْ | ḍ = ضْ | ṭ = طْ | |

## Recorded Exercise 5 — تمريـن مسجّل 5

I read: Some Alphabets connected with the three called vowel ones ā, u, i + Some silent ones — ȃqraȃ أَقْرَأُ:

| | | | | | | | |
|---|---|---|---|---|---|---|---|
| sā | سَا | su | سو | si | سي | s | سْ |
| jā | جَا | ju | جو | ji | جي | j | جْ |
| mā | مَا | mu | مو | mi | مي | m | مْ |
| lā | لاَ | lu | لو | li | لي | l | لْ |
| bā | بَا | bu | بو | bi | بي | b | بْ |
| khā | خَا | khu | خو | khi | خي | kh | خْ |
| tā | تَا | tu | تو | ti | تي | t | تْ |
| qā | قَا | qu | قو | qi | قي | q | قْ |
| kā | كَا | ku | كو | ki | كي | k | كْ، كـْ |
| ṣā | صَا | ṣu | صو | ṣi | صي | ṣ | صْ |
| nā | نَا | nu | نو | ni | ني | n | نْ |
| hā | هَا | hu | هو | hi | هي | h | هـْ |
| thā | ثَا | thu | ثو | thi | ثي | th | ثْ |
| ḥā | حَا | ḥu | حو | ḥi | حي | ḥ | حْ |
| ḍā | ضَا | ḍu | ضو | ḍi | ضي | ḍ | ضْ |
| ṭā | طَا | ṭu | طو | ṭi | طي | ṭ | طْ |
| rā | را | ru | رو | ri | ري | r | رْ |
| zā | زا | zu | زو | zi | زي | z | زْ |

## Recorded Exercise 6 تمريـن مسجّل 6

I read: Some words Formed of three alphabets with vowel sounds :أَقْرَأُ

| | | | | | | | |
|---|---|---|---|---|---|---|---|
| fataḥa | فَتَحَ | wajada | وَجَدَ | qasama | قَسَمَ | ḥamala | حَمَلَ |
| sāra | سارَ | zāra | زارَ | dāra | دارَ | ṭāra | طارَ |
| shāa̔a | شاعَ | nāma | نامَ | bāa̔a | باعَ | a̓kala | أكَلَ |
| ṣāra | صارَ | ṭāba | طابَ | dhāba | ذابَ | dhāa̔a | ذاعَ |
| sur | سُورْ | dur | دورْ | kub | كوبْ | ful | فولْ |
| nil | نِيلْ | rish | رِيشْ | mil | مِيلْ | fil | فيلْ |
| fahema | فَهِمَ | laa̔eba | لَعِبَ | samea̔a | سَمِعَ | shareba | شَرِبَ |
| qadema | قَدِمَ | ṭamea̔a | طَمِعَ | a̔alema | عَلِمَ | fareḥa | فَرِحَ |
| wojeda | وُجِدَ | qobela | قُبِلَ | fohema | فُهِمَ | a̔olema | عُلِمَ |
| māl | مالْ | jāl | جالْ | dār | دارْ | rās | راسْ |
| ṭin | طينْ | thawb | ثَوْبْ | dik | ديكْ | a̔id | عيدْ |
| kawn | كَوْنْ | tin | تينْ | nawm | نَوْمْ | yawm | يَوْمْ |
| riq | ريقْ | lawz | لَوْزْ | nur | نورْ | tut | توتْ |
| qawl | قَوْلْ | | | jawz | جَوْزْ | mawz | مَوْزْ |

## Recorded Exercise 7 — تمرين مسجّل 7

**I read:** Some words Formed of more than three alphabets with vowel sounds — أَقرأُ:

| | | | | | | | |
|---|---|---|---|---|---|---|---|
| rosum | رُسومْ | domuʿ | دُموعْ | ṣaghir | صَغيرْ | zohur | زُهورْ |
| soraʿah | سُرْعَهْ | sāʿah | ساعَهْ | zanbaq | زَنْبَقْ | jolus | جُلوسْ |
| ʿallama | عَلَّمَ | waḥḥad | وَحَّدَ | qabbala | قَبَّلَ | ṣaʿʿada | صَعَّدَ |
| qaddasa | قَدَّسَ | aṭfaʾa | أَطْفَأَ | taʾakhkhara | تَأَخَّرَ | ʾayqaḍha | أَيْقَظَ |
| ḥawwala | حَوَّلَ | wazzaʿa | وَزَّعَ | ḥabbaba | حَبَّبَ | fataḥa | فَتَحَ |
| rabiʿ | رَبيعْ | ṣahil | صَهيلْ | ʿaḍhim | عَظيمْ | raḥiq | رَحيقْ |
| nabil | نَبيلْ | basiṭ | بَسيطْ | sayyedah | سَيِّدَهْ | sayyed | سَيِّدْ |
| hāʾel | هائِلْ | bāʾeʿ | بائِعْ | qāʾed | قائِدْ | zāʾed | زائِدْ |
| ḥassān | حَسَّانْ | mofid | مُفيدْ | foṭur | فُطورْ | modir | مُديرْ |
| mariḍah | مَريضَهْ | mariḍ | مَريضْ | ṭabibah | طَبيبَهْ | ṭabib | طَبيبْ |
| sorur | سُرورْ | ḥāʾeṭ | حائِطْ | sallah | سَلَّهْ | fariq | فَريقْ |
| ladhidh | لَذيذْ | ṭawil | طَويلْ | reḥlah | رِحْلَهْ | mawʿed | مَوْعِدْ |

# 3 Formation of the Arabic Word تَرْكِيبُ الكلمةِ العَرَبيَّةِ: 3

The Arabic word is formed of connected alphabets which is different from the formation of the English one where the word is formed of disconnected letters.

This is the case with most alphabets. But there are some alphabets as: d =د, dh =ذ, r =ر, z =ز, and w =و which are written separately in some cases.

The letters = د، ذ، ر، ز are disconnected when each is the first letter of any word followed by a = ا or u = و

Examples: زارَ – راسْ – ذاقَ – دارَ – دور – روس They are also written disconnected when each one is the last letter of a word preceded by ā =ا or w =و (u = و) as the following words = عادَ – عاذَ – كازْ – كوزْ – عودْ – سورْ – دارْ – دورْ

These letters are connected with other letters in the following case such as with ءَl = ل and will be doubled then without pronouncing the al = ل as in the following words:

ءَddār الدّار - ءَrrās الرّاس - ءَdhdhib الذّيب - ءَzzād الزّاد

The w =و is also written disconnected with other alphabets when it comes as the first alphabet of any word

**Examples**: Wahaba وَهَبَ – Wafada وَفَدَ – Walad وَلَدْ

Wajada وَجَدَ – Washama وَشَمَ – Wasala وَصَلَ

# 4 Parts of the Arabic Word أَقْسام الكلمةِ العربيّةِ: 4

The Arabic Word is divided into three parts:

1 - The Verb - ảl Feål : أَلْفِعْل

2 - The Noun - ảl ẻsm : أَلإِسْمْ

3 - The Preposition/conjunction - ảl ḥarf أَلحَرْفْ

1 - The Verb - ảl feål الفِعْل denotes an action in a specified time.

a - Present - ảlmoḍāreå المُضارع as drink - yashrab : يَشْرَبْ

b - Past - ảlmāḍi الماضي as drank - shareba : شَرِبَ

c - Order - ảlảmr الأمْر as drink - ẻshrab : إشْرَبْ

N.B. Order or command is called so when it is directed from a higher person to a lower one in rank or situation. But if it is addressed from a lower person to God, for example, it will be called appeal or begging.

**Example** = O' God, forgive = يا أَللّه إِرْحَمْ - yā ảllāh ẻrḥam.

2 - The Noun - ảlẻsm الإِسْمْ denotes a name of a person, a place, an animal, a plant, or anything.

**Examples** = a boy - walad وَلَدْ , a girl - bent - بِنْتْ ,

Jack - jak جَاك , Ali - åali عَلي (Names of people).

Beirut - bayrut بَيْروت ، London - landan لَنْدَن

The Nile - annil أَلنِّيل ، The Alps - alalb الألْب

- Horn Lake - boḥayrat hurn - بُحَيْرَة هورن - (Names of places).

- dog - Kalb كَلْبْ, horse - ḥesān حِصَان (Names of animals).

- a tree - shajarah شَجَرَة, a flower - zahrah زَهْرَه (Names of Plants).

- a table - ṭāwelah طاوِلَه, a cup - fenjān فِنْجان, a pencil - qalam قَلَمْ

- a room - ghorfah غُرْفَه, milk - ḥalib حَلِيب (Names of things).

N.B. **a** - Some words are derived from verbs and are called nouns denoting actions - but with no time as: eating - åkl أكْل ,writing - ketābah كِتابَة. (compare with Gerund in English).

**b** - Or Some words denote a doer of an action as: writer - kāteb كاتِبْ, worker - åāmel - عامِلْ

**c** - Or Sometimes words denote the receiver of an ac-. tion as: written - maktub مَكْتوبْ, made - maṣnuå مَصْنوع (مَعْمول)

**d** - Or Sometimes a word denotes a kind of quality as: clean - naḍhif نَظِيف, beautiful - jamil جَمِيل....... etc.

The former four parts are called nouns in a different concept than what is discussed under article number 2 previously.

3 - Ålḥarf أَلحَرْفْ - in Arabic - is a word that has no meaning by itself. It joins words together to form a complete sense. Here are some ḥoruf حُروف which don't do the same function as in English language: from - men مِنْ, to - ělā إلى, on - ålā على, in - fi في, about - åan عَنْ, wa وَ, fa فَ, ka كَ, thomma ثُمَّ, åm أَم, åw أوْ, be بِ, .... and so on. Some function as prepositions (في ،عَنْ ،مِنْ . . .) and some function

as conjunctions (ثُمَّ ، فَ ، وَ ، أَم . . .) Now, We come to explain somethings about the verb in Arabic. The verb in Arabic may be formed of joining three or more. alphabets together.

**Examples** - Three - letter verbs: sāra سارَ zāra زارَ

dhahaba ذَهَبَ ، ṣāda صادَ ، åalema عَلِمَ

foteḥa فُتِحَ ، koteba كُتِبَ ، fohema فُهِمَ

**Examples** - More than three - letter verbs =

kātaba كاتَبَ ، kattaba كَتَّبَ ، ảảlama أَعْلَمَ

takātaba تكاتَبَ ، ẻnkasara إِنْكَسَرَ ، tafāhama تَفاهَمَ

**N.B. 1 -** There are some words in Arabic that have originally four alphabets as = zalzala زَلْزَلَ , but they are not many. (zalzala means shook in English).

**2 -** If we see some two-letter verbs in Arabic, really they are three - letter verbs, one letter being omitted as follows:

The verb sāra سارَ - which means walked in English - is a past tense verb in Arabic. The present tense of it is yasiro يَسِيرُ . The order - ảlảmr - is ser سِرْ where is the vowel letter «i» = يـ which is the second letter of the verb? It is originally Sir سِيْرْ . The vowel letter « يـ » is silent having what is called «Sokun» «ـْ» on it and the next letter to it «رْ» has also «sokun» «ـْ» on it. In Arabic, the rule is to omit the vowel letter, when two consequent letters having «sokun» «ـْ» on them meet. The same case with the past verb said: qala - قـالَ , present: yaqulo - يَقُولُ , order qol - قُلْ . The verb is originally qul قُوْلْ. Here the vowel letter «و» is silent with «sokun» «ْ» on it, and the following letter «لْ» has also «sokun» « ْ » on it and two silent letters are difficult to pronounce. There fore the vowel letter «و» is omitted.

**2 -** There are many ways of forming a verb of more than three letters from a verb of three letters originally.

I mentioned only two ways as adding «ā» after the first letter: «kātaba», or «ả» at the beginning of the verb: «ả'lama», or doubling the second letter = «kattaba», or adding «t» + «ā» as «tafāhama» (on fahema فَهِمَ), and «ẻ» + «n» as ẻnkasara (on kasara كَسَرَ).

This is sufficient for the stage, as the student may deepen and increase his knowledge of the language if he is widely interested to do so.

# 5 Arabic Sentence تَرْكيبُ الجُمْلَةِ العَرَبيَّةِ: 5

- The structure of the Arabic sentence differs from that of the English one. In English we have: Subject + Verb or

Subject + Verb + Complement (Object or other phrases or words).

**Examples:** (a) The boy drank (b) the boy drank milk. (c) the book is useful.

For example «a» we have the Arabic sentence

شَرِبَ الوَلَدُ . Shareba ȃl walado

For example «b» we say in Arabic

شَرِبَ الوَلَدُ الحليبَ . Shareba ȃl walado ȃl ḥaliba

For The example «c» we say in Arabic

الكتابُ مفيدٌ . ȃl Ketabo mofidon

**Notes:** 1- The verb precedes its subject in the Arabic sentence.

2- The verb must agree with its subject in gender, but Not In Number.

For the English sentence: The girl drank, we say in Arabic:

Sharebat ả̉l bento شَرِبتْ البِنْتُ .

We added «t» at the end of the past verb for the female subject.

drank = shareba شَرِبَ – boy = walad وَلَدْ – milk = halib حَليبْ

book = ketāb كِتابْ – useful = mofid مُفيدْ – girl = bent بِنْتْ

For the English sentences: «the boys drank, the girls drank» we say in Arabic: shareba ả̉l waladān (for two) شَرِبَ ألوَلْدانِ .

and shareba ả̉l ả̉wlado (for more than two) شَرِبَ ألأوْلادُ .

**Notice** **that the verb** remained singular with **its** plural subject.

- In such a sentence: «The garden is beautiful»,

we say in Arabic:ả̉l bostāno jamilon البُستانُ جَميلٌ .

(No Verb in the sentence but a noun and another word to complete the meaning).

We say in English: «The boys are active». In Arabic,

We say = ả̉l ả̉wlādo nashitun (No Verb) الأولادُ نشيطونَ .

(Here, the predicate agreed with the subject in number and in gender. We add «un» for the plural masculine.)

We say in English. «The girls are active.

«In Arabic, we say: al banato nashitat (No Verb) البَناتُ نشيطاتٌ.

**Notice Here** the predicate agreed with the subject in number - by adding «āt» for the plural female - and it also agreed with the subject in gender.

## Recorded Exercise 8 — تمـريــن مسجّل 8

I read: أَقْرأُ:

1 – طارَ العُصْفُورُ عن الشَّجَرَةِ.

2 – يَصيدُ الصَّيَّادُ السَّمكَ.

3 – سَمِعَ عادِلُ الخَبَرَ.

4 – يَلْعَبُ الأوْلادُ بِالمَلْعَبِ.

5 – قَطَفتِ البِنْتُ الوَرْدَ.

6 – رَسَمَ أَحْمَدُ صورةً.

7 – فَحصَ الطَّبيبُ المَريضَ.

8 – ألفيلُ حَيَوانٌ ضَخْمٌ.

---

boys = (dual + singular)= waladàn + ảwlàd وَلَدان + أوْلاد

garden = bostàn بُسْتان – beautiful = jamil جَميل

active = nashiṭ نَشِيط

Arabic Alphabets are two kinds concerning their pronunciation with «ål». They are what we call the Moon Alphabets: «Al ḥoruf al qamareyah» - and what we call Sun Alphabets: «al ḥoruf al shamsey-ah»

***The Moon Alphabets are***

b = ب, j = ج, ḥ = ح, kh = خ, å = ع, gh = غ, f = ف, q = ق, ā = ا
k = ك, m = م, h = هـ, w = و, y = ي, and «al hamzeh», (14 in number)

***The Sun Alphabets are :***

t = ت, th = ث, d = د, dh = ذ, r = ر, z = ز, s = س, sh = ش,
ṣ = ص, ḍ = ض, ṭ = ط, ḍh = ظ, l = ل, n = ن (14 in number)

The «ảl» is pronounced clearly with the Moon Alphabets as the Arabic word ảl qamar أَلْقمر

ảl bāb وأَلْبابْ ảl jamal وأَلْجَمَلْ ảl faras أَلفَرَسْ

The letter «ảl» أل - this «L» ل is not pronounced with the sun Alphabets, and in this case the sun letter is doubled as in: ảl shams which is pronounced «sh» ash shams by doubling the letter = ش ، الشَّمْس

اللَّبَنُ = a̓llaban والسَّمَكُ = a̓ssamak ، الدَّارُ = a̓ddar

(Note= the «l» ل is written but not pronounced).

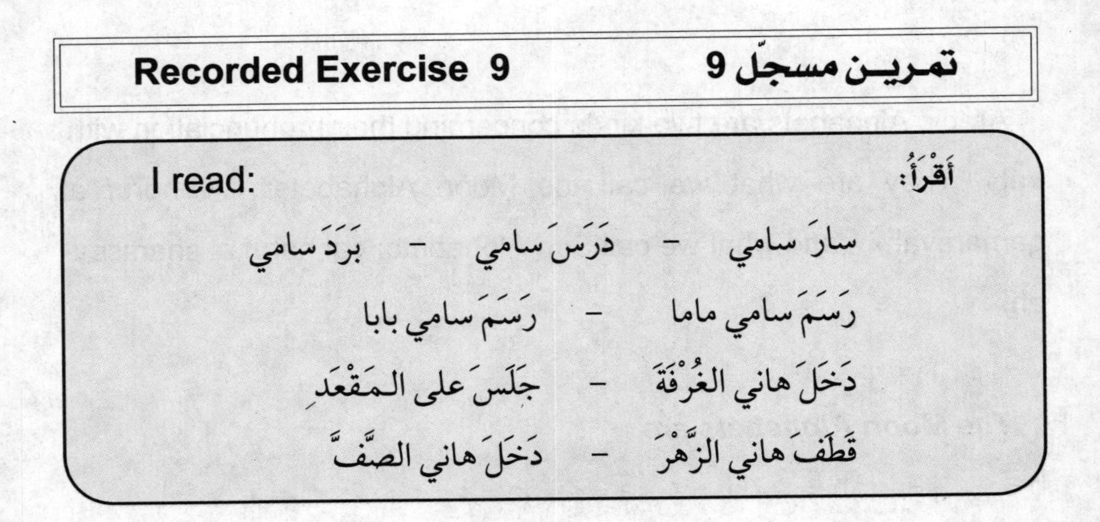

**Recorded Exercise 9** **تمـريـن مسجّل 9**

I read: **أَقْرَأُ:**

سارَ سامي – دَرَسَ سامي – بَرَدَ سامي

رَسَمَ سامي ماما – رَسَمَ سامي بابا

دَخَلَ هاني الغُرْفَةَ – جَلَسَ على المَقْعَدِ

قَطَفَ هاني الزَّهْرَ – دَخَلَ هاني الصَّفَّ

---

moon = qamar قَمَر – sun = shams شَمْس

door = bab باب – camel = jamal جَمَل

Yog (h) urt = laban لَبَن

# 7 Adjective — الصِّفَة

The adjective in English comes before the noun.

In Arabic, an adjective comes after the noun and should agree with this noun in <u>number</u>, <u>gender</u> and <u>case</u>. Examples:

1. ȇshtara l walado l ketāba al jadida : إشترى الوَلَدُ الكتابَ الجَديدَ .

(book: singular, object with ´ on the last letter. The addjective is the same).

2. ȇshtara l walado l ketabayn l jadidayn : إشْتَرى الوَلَدُ الكتابَيْن الجديدَيْن .

3. qaraȃ l walado l qeṣṣata l qaṣirata: قَرأ الولدُ القصّةَ القَصيرة .

4. qaraȃ l walado l qeṣṣatayn l qaṣiratayn: قَرأ الولدُ القِصَّتينِ القصيرتَيْنِ .

• In example number 2, the word «ȃl ketābayn» is dual, masculine and object. The adjective «ȃl jadidayn» agreed with it.

• In example 3, «ȃl qeṣṣata» is singular. feminine and object, the adjective agreed with it (i.e. with the qualified noun).

And so on with the plural noun which will be qualified by an adjective.

«Ḥaḍara l ȃwlado nnashitun»: حضرَ الأولادُ النَشيطونَ .

## Unrecorded Exercise 10     تمرين غير مسجّل 10

**Fill in the blank with the correct adjective in brackets.**

1. قطفَ الولدُ الوَرْدَةَ ......................... (جميل)
2. في القَفَصِ عُصْفوران ......................... (صغير)
3. كَسَرَ سامرُ القَلَمَيْنِ ......................... (كبير)
4. في المْدرَسةُ مُعَلِّمونَ ......................... (نشيط)
5. اشترى الوَلَدُ كِتابَيْنِ ......................... (قديم)
6. سَقَطتِ الأوْراقُ ......................... (الأصفر)
7. كَتَبَ الوَلَدُ الفروضَ ......................... (الجديد)
8. صَفَّقَ الصَّفُ للطّالِباتِ ......................... (الذّكيّة)

---

walked = sāra سارَ (مشى) – studied = darasa دَرَسَ

got cold = barada بَرَدَ – drew = rasama رَسَمَ

sat = jalasa جَلَسَ – on = ʿālā على – to = ʾelā إلى

desk = maqaad مَقْعدٌ – picked = qatafa قَطَفَ

flower = zahrah زَهْرَه – class = saff صَفْ

# 8 Interrogation - Question الإسْتِفْهام

| | |
|---|---|
| Man safara èlā london? | مَنْ سافرَ إلى لَنْدَن؟ |
| Mādhā ảkala Ả'ḥmad? | ماذا أكلَ أحْمدُ؟ |
| Le mādhā sāfara Ả'ḥmad? | لماذا سافرَ أحْمَدُ؟ |
| Mata sāfara Ả'ḥmad? | مَتى سافرَ أحْمَدُ؟ |
| Ả'yna sāfara Ả'ḥmad | أيْنَ سافرَ أحْمَدُ؟ |
| Kayfa ḥalo Ả'ḥmad? | كَيْفَ حالُ أحْمَدُ؟ |

**Note:** We ask about a person by «man» = Who?

We ask about a thing by «mādhā» = What?

We ask about the reason by «lemādhā» = Why?

We ask about the time by «matā» = When?

We ask about the place by «ả'yna» = Where?

We ask about the manner by kayfa = How?

If the answer of a question may be «yes» or «no», we ask by «hal» before a verb as:

hal safara Ả'ḥmad? هَلْ سافرَ أحْمَدُ؟

The answer may be yes = «naảm», or no = «Lā»

travelled = safara سَافرَ

did = hal هَلْ

# 9 Present Tense Formation

# تَكْوِين الفِعْلِ المُضَارِع

The verbs given in the previous pages were in the past tense. Now we want to know how to build up the present tense.

- Speaking about one self, one puts «ả» or «ỏ» before the past verb as «ảlảabo» = أَلْعَبُ – «ỏsāfero» = أُسافِرُ – «ảktobo» = أكْتُبُ – «ả shrabo» = أَشْرَبُ
- Speaking about ourselves, we put «n′» or «n'» before the past verb as: «nalảabo» = نَلْعَبُ – «nosāfero» = نُسافِرُ – «naktobo» = نكْتُبُ – «nashrabo» = نَشْرَبُ
- When we speak about a third person singular and masculine we put «ya» before the past verb as «yashrabo» = يَشْرَبُ – «yalảabo» - يَلْعَبُ
- We add «ya + un» for plural masculine nouns as masculine noun as «yashrabun » = (هُم) يَشْرَبُونَ
- We add «ya + an» for dual «yashraban» = (هُما) يَشْرَبان

«Yalảabun» = (هم) يلْعبون

«Yalảaban» = (هُما) يلْعَبان

- We add «t»before the past verb when we speak about:

**(a)** a second person singular and masculine as:

«Tashrabo» = (أنت) تَشْرَبُ – «Talảabo» = (أنت) تلعَبُ

«Tosâfero» (أنت) تُسافرُ

**(b)** a third person singular and feminine as in item «a» above.

هيَ تشْرَبُ – هيَ تَلْعَبُ – هي تُسافرُ

- We add «t» and «in» to the past verb when its doer of action is second person singular and feminine as:

«Talʿaabin» = (أنتِ) تَلْعَبين – «Tashrabin» – (أنتِ) تَشْرَبين

drink = Yashrab . . . يَشْرَب/ أَشْرَبُ . – play = Yalʿaab . . . نَلْعَب/ يَلْعَب .

- We add «t» + «un» to the verb when its doer of action is second person plural and masculine as:

«talʿaabun» = (أنتم) تَلْعَبون – «to sāferun» = (أنتم) تُسافِرون

- We add «t» + «n» to the past verb when its doer of action is second person plural and Feminine as:

«talʿaabna» = (أنْتُنَّ) تَلْعَبْنَ – «tashrabna» = (أنتنَّ) تَشْرَبْنَ

«to sāferna» = (أنْتُنّ) تُسافِرْنَ

- We add «t» + «an» to the verb when its doer of action is second person dual masculine and to third person dual feminine as.

«tashrabān» = (أنْتُما) تَشْرَبان

«talʿaabān» = (أنْتُما) تَلْعَبان

«tosāferān» = (أنْتُما) تُسافران

and «tashrabān» = هُما تَشْرَبان (for dual Feminine)

«talʿaabān» = هُما تَلْعَبَان (for dual Feminine)

ả**ḍḍ**amāẻr (pronouns) are many kinds. We shall deal with the necessary kinds for this stage.

Here are two kinds: the connected and the disconnected,

«ảl monfaṣelah» The Disconnected أ- الـمُنْفَصِلَة .

| First Person | Second Person | Third Person |
|---|---|---|
| Mas + Fem.Sing أنا | Masc.Sing أنتَ | Masc.Sing هُوَ |
| Mas + Fem.Plur نَحْنُ | Masc.Dual أَنْتُما | Masc.Dual هُما |
| | Masc.Plur أَنْتُم | Masc.Plur هُمْ |
| | Fem.Sing أَنْتِ | Fem.Sing هيَ |
| | Fem.Dual أَنْتما | Fem.Dual هُما |
| | Fem. Plur أَنْتُنَّ | Fem.Plur هُنَّ |

ب- الضمائر المتّصلة Connected

«تُ» في كَتَبْتُ = «Katabto» - Speaker

تَ في كَتَبْتَ = «Katabta» Addressed - Masculine (sing).

تِ في كَتَبْتِ = «Katabte» Addressed-Feminine (sing).

نا في كَتَبْنا = «Katabna» 1 st Person (plur) Masc. + Fem.

3rd. Person (plur) Fem. «Katabna» = في كَتَبْنَ ن

3rd. Person (Dual) Masc. «Katabā» = في كَتَبَا ا

3rd. Person (Dual) Fem. «Katabatā» = في كَتَبَتَا

There are other pronouns which will be dealt with in chapter eleven

## تَصْرِيفُ الماضي والمُضارِعُ والأَمْر مَعَ الضَّمائِرِ

**Conjugation of the Present, Past and Order with the Pronouns:**

| Order «Ỏktob» | | Present Verb «Yaktobo» | | Past Verb «Kataba» | | |
|---|---|---|---|---|---|---|
| — | | Yaktobo | يَكْتُبُ | Kataba | كَتَبَ | هُوَ |
| — | | Yaktobān | يَكْتُبان | Katabā | كَتَبَا | هُما |
| — | | Yaktobun | يَكْتُبُون | Katabu | كَتَبوا | هُمْ |
| — | | Taktobo | تَكْتُبُ | Katabat | كَتَبَت | هيَ |
| — | | Taktobāne | تَكْتُبَان | Katabatā | كَتَبَتا | هُما |
| — | | Yaktobna | يَكْتُبْنَ | Katabna | كَتَبْنَ | هُنَّ |
| ỏktob | أكْتُبْ | Taktobō | تَكْتُبُ | Katabta | كَتَبْتَ | أَنْتَ |
| ỏktoba | أُكْتُبا | Taktobane | تَكْتُبَان | Katabtomā | كَتَبْتُما | أنْتُما |
| ỏktobū | أكْتُبوا | Taktobuna | تَكْتُبونَ | Katabtom | كَتَبْتُم | أنْتُم |
| ỏktobi | أكْتُبي | Taktobina | تَكْتُبينَ | Katabte | كَتَبْتِ | أنْتِ |
| ỏktoba | أكْتُبا | Taktobāne | تَكْتُبان | Katabtomā | كَتَبْتُما | أنْتُما |
| ỏktobna | أكْتُبْنَ | Taktobna | تَكْتُبْنَ | Katabtunna | كَتَبْتُنَّ | أنْتُنَّ |
| — | | Ảktobo | أَكْتُبُ | Katabto | كَتَبْتُ | أنا |
| — | | Naktobo | نَكْتُبُ | Katabnā | كَتَبْنَا | نَحْنُ |

Write = Yaktobo يَكْتُبُ – Wrote = Kataba كَتَبَ

Future Tense Verb which means «ảl Mostaqbal» المُسْتَقبَل

is formed in Arabic by adding «s» = س, or «sawfa» = سَوْفَ

to the present verb. The future verb will/shall buy is expressed

sawfa ảshtari = سَوْفَ أشْتَري ، Saảshtari = . . . . . . . سَأشْتَري

## Pronouns in the Objective case ج- الضَّمائِرُ المُتَّصِلَةُ في النَّصْبِ والجَرِّ

ي، كَ، ه، نا .

my book : كتابي = ketābi – your book : كتَابَكَ = Ketābaka

his book : كتابُهُ = Ketaboho – Her book : كتَابُها = Ketabohā

their books : كُتُبهم = Kotobohom – our books : كُتُبُنا = Kotobonā

y: for the speaker (1st. person) – ي

K: for the addressed (2nd. person/s) – ك، كم

h/h+m: for the absentee/s (3 rd. person/s) – ـه، ـها

nā: for the speakers (1st. Persons) – نا

- These Pronouns may be connected with verbs also as: Faḥaṣa = فحص

When connected with the pronouns ي، ك، ـه، نا in order will be

Faḥaṣani = فَحَصَني by adding «n» = ن with the y = ي

Faḥaṣaka = فَحَصَك - Faḥaṣaho = فَحَصَهُ

Faḥaṣahā = فَحَصَها - Faḥaṣanā = فَصَحنا

## Recorded Exercise 11 — تمرين مسجّل 11

1. أنا أكْتبُ فُروضي
2. هي تَكتُبُ فُروضَها
3. أنتَ تَكْتُبُ فُروضَكَ
4. أنْتمْ تكْتبونَ فُروضَكُمْ
5. أنتِ تَكْتبينَ فُروضَكِ
6. أنتُما تَكْتُبانِ فُروضَكُماَ
7. أنتُنَّ تَكْتُبْنَ فروضَكُنَّ
8. نَحْنُ كَتَبْنا فُروضَنا
9. هُما تَكْتُبانِ فُروضَهما (بنتان)
10. هُما يَكتُبانِ فرُوضَهُما (ولدان)
11. طارَ الطّائِرُ في السَّماءِ.
12. يَعيشُ الأسَدُ في الغابَةِ.
13. لَبِسَ الولَدُ القَميصَ.

## Recorded Exercise 12 — تمرين مسجّل 12

1. ماذا رَسَمَ طارِقْ؟
2. أينَ سافرَ أَحْمَدُ؟
3. هلْ قَطَفَ سمير ُالأزْهارَ؟
4. كَيفَ الطَّقسُ اليوْمَ؟
5. مَنْ ساعَدَ الفقيرَ؟
6. كَمْ قَبَضَ الموَظَّفُ؟
7. لماذا ربَطَ المُسافِرُ الحِزامَ؟
8. حَطَّتِ الطّائِرَةُ على الأَرْضِ.

---

buy = âshtari أشْتَري - book = ketāb - examine, test = yafḥaṣ يَفْحَص - duty = farḍ فَرْض

The present verb: ảlmoḍareẚ has different vowel sounds on its last letter. It usually has the vowel sound «o» - ḍammah - on the last letter unless it is preceded by certain articles:

«yaṣiḥo»..... يَصيحُ الدّيكُ

«Yoḥebbo»..... يُحِبُّ الأطْفالُ الحَليب

If this verb is preceded by <u>some</u> articles, the vowel sound will change as in following cases:

(a) if «lam» = لم or «lā» precedes this verb, there will be no vowel sound on the last letter. i.e. there will be what is called in Arabic «sokun» = ـْـ سكونْ

**<u>Example</u>:** lam yaḍḥa<u>k</u> walid. لَمْ يَضْحكْ وليد .

«Lā» takdhe<u>b</u> (order in the negative) لا تكْذِبْ.

(b) If «ản» = أنْ or «lan» = لَنْ or «kay» = كَيْ

precedes this verb, the vowel sound on the last letter will be «a» = ـَـ فَتْحَه

**<u>Example</u>:** ỏrid<u>o</u> <u>ản</u> ảsba<u>ḥa</u>. أريدُ <u>أنْ</u> أسْبحَ.

**<u>Example:</u>** lan yakdheba Salim. لَنْ يكْذِبَ سَليم.

**<u>Exampe:</u>** naảkol<u>o</u> <u>kay</u> naẚish<u>a</u>. نَأكلُ <u>كَي</u> نَعيشَ.

**<u>Note:</u>** If the present verb ends with any of the vowel letters ا، و، ي and is peceded by «lam» or «la», the vowel letter must be omitted.

**Examples** :

«lam ảra» (it was ảrā) لَمْ أرَ – أرى الغَيْمَ

«lam yabke» (it was yabki) لَمْ يَبْكِ – يَبْكي الولدُ

«lam yarjo» (it was yarju) لَمْ يَرْجُ – يَرْجو

(c) If the present verb is connected with the letter n = «ن» at the end ,

the last letter of the verb will be silent. This «n» is called in Arabic

«nun ảnnesẩ» نون النّساء

It means that the verb expresses the plural feminine doer of the action, when we say in English «The women clean the clothes», we express that in Arabic: ảnnesẩ yaghselna lmalābesa. النِّساءُ يَغْسلْنَ الملابسَ

---

cry = yaşiḥ يَصيح - cock = dik دِيك - milk = ḥalib حَليب

like = yoḥebb يُحِبّ - laugh = yaḍḥak = يَضْحَك - lie = yakdheb يكْذِب

want = ổrid أريد - swim = yasbaḥ يَسْبَح - eat = yaảkol يَأكُل

live = naaish نَعيش - cry, weep = yabki يَبْكي - beg = yarju يَرْجو

wash, clean = yaghsel يَغْسل

# 12 Past Tense and Imperative Mood

# الـفِـعْـلُ الـمـاضـي وفِـعْـلُ الأمْـر 12

I - The vowel sound on the last letter of the past verb is what we call in Arabic «fatḥa» a, unless the past verb is connected with some pronouns.

The past verb «faṭaha», has the «a» َ - «fataḥa» فَتحَ on its last letter.

Also «labesa» has «a» َ - «labesa» لَبسَ on the last letter.

- (a) When we annex the pronoun «w» = و to it,

the vowel on the letter will be «u» = «fataḥu» فَتحُوا

The Same case will be «labesụ» = لبِسوا

and so on will any past verb with «u» annexed to it.

- (b) When we annex the pronouns «to», «ta», «te» تُ، تَ، تِ

to the verb, the last letter of the verb will be silent - no vowel sound on it, (it will have sokun).

فَتحَ = فتَحِتْتُ، فَتَحِتْتَ ، فَتَحِتْتِ

fataḥa = fataḥto (for the speaker) and

fataḥta (for the second person masculine)

fataḥte (for the second person feminine)

II - The Imperative Mood (ȃmr) has no vowel sound on its last letter. When we want to ask the second person masculine to do any thing, we say in Arabic إفْتَحْ = eftah - or إلْبسْ = elbas...

(a) when asking the dual (common gender), we say

إفْتَحا = ẻftaḥā - and إِلْبَسا = ẻlbasā.....

(b) when ordering - asking - the plural masculine, we say إفتحوا = eftaḥu

إفْتَحوا = ẻftaḥu and إلبَسْوا = ẻlbasu.....

When ordering the plural feminine, we say

إفْتَحْنَ = ẻftaḥna and إلْبَسْنَ = ẻlbasna.....

(c) Omit the last vowel letter in these cases: (order)

يَرْجو = أُرْجُ ỏrjo – يَرْمي = إرْمِ ẻrme – يَبْقى = إبْقَ ẻbqa

| **Recorded Exercise 13** | **تمـريـن مسجّل 13** |
| --- | --- |

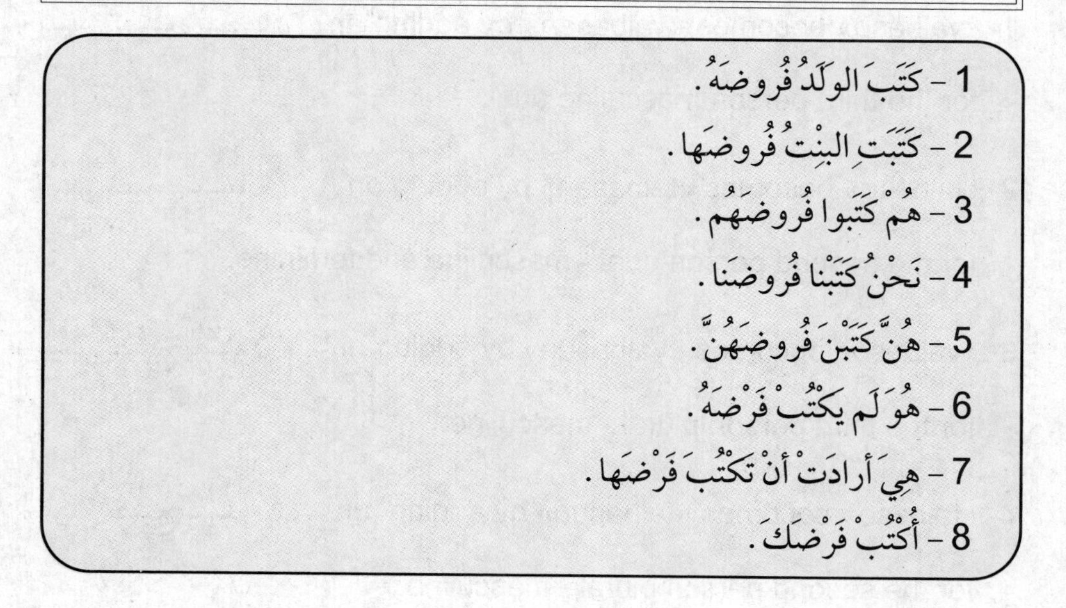

1 - كَتَبَ الوَلَدُ فُروضَهُ .

2 - كَتَبَتِ البِنْتُ فُروضَها .

3 - هُمْ كَتَبوا فُروضَهُم .

4 - نَحْنُ كَتَبْنا فُروضَنا .

5 - هُنَّ كَتَبْنَ فُروضَهُنَّ .

6 - هُوَ لَم يكْتُبْ فَرْضَهُ .

7 - هِيَ أرادَتْ أنْ تكْتُبَ فَرْضَها .

8 - أُكْتُبْ فَرْضَكَ .

---

opened = fataḥa فَتَحَ

# 13 The Five Verbs - Characteristics الأَفْعالُ الخَمْسَةُ إِعْرابُها 13

The Following present verbs are called the five verbs. They are the simple present verb connected with the following pronouns forming five forms of present verbs.

«ā» for the dual of common gender (2nd + 3rd person) ألفُ الاثْنَين

«u» for the plural masculine (2nd + 3rd person) واوُ الجماعة

«i» for the 2nd person feminine only. ياءُ المُخاطَبَة

1- «yalbaso» becomes «yalbasān» by adding"ān" يَلْبَسُ تصبح يَلْبَسان
for the third person masculine dual.

2- «talbaso» becomes «talbasān» by adding"ān" تَلْبَسُ تُصْبِحَ تَلْبَسان
for the second person dual - masculine and feminine.

3- «yalbaso» becomes «yalbasun» by adding"un" يَلْبَسُ تُصْبِح يَلْبَسون
for the third person plural - masculine.

4- «talbaso» becomes «talbasun» by adding "un" تَلْبَسُ تُصْبِح تَلْبَسون
for the second person plural - masculine.

5- «Talbaso» becomes «talbasin» by adding"in" تَلْبَسُ تُصبِح تَلْبَسين
for the second person feminine.

• These verbs when preceded by «lam», «lā», «ȃn», «lan» and «kay» will be without the «n» at the end.

**Examples:** lam yalbasā . . . لَمْ يَلْبَسا

lā talbasu . . . لا تَلْبَسوا

ȃn yalbasā . . . أنْ يَلْبَسا

lan talbasi . . . لَنْ تَلْبَسي

| **Recorded Exercise 14** | **تمـريـن مسجّل 14** |
|---|---|

أقْـرَأ

1 - أَلأَطْفالُ يُحِبّونَ الحَلْوَى

2 - أَلْعُمّالُ يَقْطِفونَ العِنَبَ.

3 - أَرادوا أنْ يَخْرُجوا لِلنُّزهَةِ.

4 - أَلأَهْلُ لَمْ يَسمَحوا لَهُمْ.

5 - لا تَأْكُلوا قَبْلَ أنْ تَغْسِلوا أيْديكُمْ.

6 - ساعِدوا الضَّعيفَ.

7 - أَجيبا عَنِ السُّؤالْ.

8 - إبْحَثي عَنِ الحَلّ.

---

dress = yalbas, talbas . . . . يَلْبَس/ تَلْبَس

# 14 Active and Passive — المَعْلُومْ والمَجْهولْ 14

The passive voice «ȃlmajhul» is built up from a transitive verb. It is very easy in Arabic since we have only two kinds of verbs which may be changed into the Passive.

Let us take the Past verb in the following sentence:

The boy broke the pencil = kasara l walado l qalama كَسرَ الوَلدُ القلمَ.

The subject - doer of the action - in Arabic has the vowel sound «o» which is known as «ḍammah» - on the last letter: الولدُ.

The object has the vowel sound «a» - which is called «fatḥah» in Arabic - on the last letter : القلمَ.

a- How do we make the passive of the past verb?

we put «o» ḍammah - on the first letter, and «e» - kasrah - on the last but one, and omit the subject replacing the object in its place calling it in this case the acting doer of the action - naȇb l fāˁel – نائبُ الفاعِل

This acting doer of the action will have «o» - ḍammah - on its last letter.

The sentence will be in the passive kosera l qalamo: كُسِرَ القَلَمُ

b - How do we form the passive of the Present verb?

Consider the following :

**example** = يكْسرُ الْولَدُ القلمَ.

We put «o» - ḍammah - on the first letter and «a» - fatḥah - on the last but one following the same procedure as above.

The sentence will be in the passive

yoksaro l qalamo      يُكْسَرُ القلَمُ .

## Unrecorded Exercise 15      تمرين غير مسجّل 15

● حوّل إلى المَجْهول **Change into the passive**

1- شَرِبَ الْوَلَدُ الحَليبَ ..........

2- يَشْرَبُ الوَلَدُ الحَليبَ ..........

3- سَمِعَ المُعَلّمُ الصَّوْتَ ..........

4- يَسْمَعُ المُعَلِّمُ الصَّوْتَ ..........

---

break = yaksero يَكْسِرُ - broke = kasara كَسَرَ - pencil = qalam قَلَمْ

teacher = moaallem مُعَلّم – sound = sawt صَوْت

water = ma ماء – fire = nar نار – lessons = dorus دُروس

## Recorded Exercise 16 تمـريـن مسجّل 16

أقْرأ :

1. الوَلَدانِ يَشْرَبان الماءَ.
2. الوَلَدانِ لَمْ يَشْرَبا الماءَ.
3. الأَوْلادُ يَلْعَبونَ
4. لا تَلْعَبوا بالنَّارِ.
5. التَّلاميذُ يَدْرُسونَ دروسَهُمْ.
6. أرادَ التَّلاميذُ أنْ يَدْرسوا دُروسَهُمْ.

## Unrecorded Exercise 17 تمرين غير مسجّل 17

- أمْلأُ الفَراغ بالكَلِمَةِ الصَّحيحَةِ Fill in the blank with the correct word

1. أرادَ الأَوْلادُ أنْ . . . . (يشربون)
2. خَرَجوا كَيْ . . . . (يلعبون)
3. دَرَسَا كَيْ . . . . . (ينجحان)
4. لَمْ . . . . فرُوضَهُم. (يكتبون)
5. لِماذا لَمْ . . . . الدّواءَ ؟ (تأخذين)
6. الصَّيّادون . . . . السَّمكَ. (يصيد)
7. العامِلانِ . . . . في الحَقْلِ. (يعمل)
8. أنْتِ . . . . الغُرْفةَ كُلَّ يَوم. (تنظّف)

---

went out = kharaja خَرَجَ – take = yaْkhodh يَأخُذ

medicine = dawā دَواء – hunter - ṣayyad صَيّاد

labourer = ʿāmel عامِلْ – work = yaʿmal يَعْمَلْ

field = ḥaql حَقْل – clean = yonaḍhef يُنَظِّف – room = ghorfah غُرْفَه

## 15 Vowel sounds and Nouns — عَلامـاتُ الإعْـراب في الأسْماء

Many names in Arabic have different vowel sounds on the last letter. This is according to their function in the sentence.

**I -** The vowel sound «o»- ḍammah ـُـ الضَّمَّه is in such cases:

a- The doer of the action = ẚl fāẚel الفاعل

**Example:** jalasa l walado جَلَسَ الوَلَدُ

b- The acting doer of the action: «nāẚb ẚlfāẚel»: نائبْ الفاْعل

**Example**: kosera zzojājo (the glass was broken) كُسـرَ الزُّجـاجُ

c- The subject and the predicate when both are noun words = المُبْتَدأ والخَبَرْ

**Example:** The book is useful الكِتابُ مُفيدٌ

al ketābo mofidon (o+o = on in pronunciation)

There are other cases of this kind which will be dealt with in other chapters.

**II -** The vowel sound «a» - fatḥah ـَـ الفَتْحة is in such cases:

a- On the last letter of the object.

Ṣanaẚate l ommo l kaẚka صَنَعتِ الأُمُّ الكَعْكَ

---

sat: jalasa = جَلَسَ - glass: zojāj = زُجَاج

make: يَصْنَع = yaṣnaẚ - made : صَنَع - cakes : كَعْك = kaẚk

= The mother made the cakes. Where the subject - doer of the action «ʾal ʾommo» - has ḍammah ـُـ on the last letter;

and the object ʾalkaʿaka has fatḥah ـَـ on the last letter.

b - On the last letter of the word which is called in Arabic «ʾal ḥāl» والحال

and in English adverb of manner.

**Example:** ḥaḍara ṣṣadiqo bākeran حَضرَ الصَّديقُ باكِراً

the friend came early «bākeran» is called «ḥāl» in Arabic, and

should have double «ā» that is «fāthatan» on the last letter.

(the ـً are on the «ā» after the «r»)

**Note:** The last letter of a noun has two vowel sounds of any kind if it has no «al» - no «the» .

**Examples:** man - friend - school رَجُلٌ - صديقًا - مَدْرَسةٍ

«rajolon» - «Ṣadiqan» - «madrasaten»

**Example:** mashā l walado mosreʿan . مَشى الوَلَدُ مُسْرِعًا

The boy walked quickly .

«mosreʿan» is «ʾal ḥāl» in Arabic with «fatḥatan» on the last letter. (The ـً are put on «ā» added to any last letter of the «alphabets in these cases except for the letter «ـة» - «ة»

- The ـً appears on this letter without adding «ā» - ا .

- Some adverbs of time or place are included in this rule.

**III-** The vowel sound «kasrah» ـِ «e» -كَسْرَه- is in such cases:

a- When the noun is in the genetive case i.e. مُضاف إلَيْه

When another noun precedes another noun and the second noun makes the first one clear.

**Example:** the teacher's table طاوِلَةُ الْمُعَلِّمِ

The noun «teacher's» was added to another noun «table» - this noun is what we call in Arabic «ảl moḍāf ẻlayhe» . الْمُضافِ إلَيْهِ

This noun takes « ـِ Kasrah» - «e» - on the last letter.

**Examples:** كُتُبُ الأَوْلادِ – حَديقَةُ البَيْتِ

**Note:** The first noun, which is called al «moḍāf» must have neither «nun» -ن-, nor «tanwin» ( ـٌ ـً ـٍ )

b - When the noun is preceded by a preposition.

Here are some prepositions:

بعض حروف الجّر: مِنْ – إلى – عَنْ – عَلى – في – ب – ل . . .

**Example:** He went out <u>from</u> the village <u>to</u> the city.

خَرَجَ مِنَ القَرْيَةِ إلى المَدينَةِ.

The prepositions «من» ، «إلى» preceded the nouns: القَرْيَةِ ، المدينَةِ

So the nouns had «kasrah» on the last letter. We say that القريةِ is governed by مِن and having the vowel sound «kasrah» - «e» on the last letter.

---

preposition : حَرْف جَرّ – city: مَدينَة - village: قَرْيَة - pen: قَلم حِبْر

نَقول : القريةِ إسْمٌ مَجْرُور بحَرْفِ الجَرّ مِن وعَلامةُ الجرّ الكَسْرة في آخِره .

**Example**: مِثال - We write with the pen. نكْتُبُ بِالقَلمِ

**Example**: مِثال - The book is for Samir. الكِتَابُ لِسَمير

**IV** (a) The dual noun «المثَنَّى» has «ان» instead of ـُـ

**Example**: مثال The two teachers came حَضرَ المُعَلِّمانِ

المعلمان : فاعِل للفِعْل «حَضرَ» مرْفوع وعَلامةُ الرّفعِ «ألِفْ وَنون» .

(b) **Example** مثال I saw the two teachers. رأيْتُ المعلمَيْنِ

The dual noun has «ين» when it is object of a transitive verb.

We express that in Arabic:

المعلَميْن : مَفْعول بهِ للفِعْلِ مَنْصوب وعَلامةُ النَّصْبِ «الياء والنون» .

(c) The dual noun has also «ين» when it is preceded by a preposition:

The man looked at the two ducks . نَظرَ الرَّجُلُ إلى البطَّتَيْنِ

نقول : البطتَيْن مَجْرور بِحَرَفِ الجَرّ «إلى» وعَلامةُ الجّر «أَلياء والنُّون» .

**V -** There is a kind of plural in Arabic called:

Jamâ al modhakkar âssālem جَمْعُ المُذَكّرِ السَّالِم

This plural is formed from a singular masculine noun by adding «un» or «in» to the singular.

سَبّاح : سَبّاحون/ سَبّاحِين

---

swim, swam سَبَح ، يَسْبَح – swimmer سَبّاح - looked at نَظَر إلى - duck بَطَّة

(a) The swimmers swam نقول سَبَح السَّباحون .

(b) نَظَرتُ إلى السبَّاحِين - رَأيْتُ السَبَّاحِين .

I looked at the swimmers - I saw the swimmers. The «swimmers» is preceded by a preposition «at» «إلى» and is the object of the verb saw رأيتُ and In the two cases it has «ين». We express that in Arabic.

السَّبَّاحين : مَجْرور بحَرْف الجرّ «إلى» وعلامَةُ الجرّ «الياء والنُّون» .

السبَّاحين : مَفْعول بهِ للفعْل رأى مَنْصوب وعَلامَةُ النَّصْبِ «ألْياء والنُّون» .

**VI-** There are what we call in Arabic the «Five Nouns»

الأسْماء الخَمْسه - وهي أبٌ - أخٌ - حمٌ - فو - ذو

and they have some rules.

husband's/wife's father = حمٌ - brother = أخْ - father = أبْ

of/owner of = ذو - mouth = فو

These nouns, when are «moḍāf», and in the subjective case حَالةُ الرَّفْع have «u» - «و» as: your father came: جاء أبوكَ

نقول أبو : فاعِل للفِعْل جاء مَرفوع وعَلاَمَةُ الرَّفْع «الواو» . ونَقول رَأيْتُ أباكَ - «أبا» مَفْعول به للفِعْل «رأى» مَنْصوب وعَلاَمَةُ النَّصْبِ «الألف» .

ونقولَ نظرْتُ إلى أبيكَ - «أبي» مَجْرور بِحَرْفِ الجرّ «إلى» وعَلاَمَةُ الجرّ «الياء» .

---

tree: شَجَرَة - studious: مُجْتَهد (ة)

plant : يَزْرَع - planted : زَرع - farmer : فَلاّح

ground: أرْض - sky: سماء - clear : صافية

money: نقُود، مال - bought: اشْتَرَى - give, gave: يُعْطي ، أعْطَى

successful: ناجح - prize: جائزَة

**VII-** There is also a plural called «jamȧ ȧl moȧnnath ȧl sālem»

مُعَلِّمات – مُجْتَهِداتِ – نَظيفات – شَجَرات :as

Such nouns take «e» - كَسْرَه ــِ when they are objects, but not «a» - fathah ــَ and In the subjective case they have «o» - ḍammah ــُ as usual.

**Note:** This plural is formed by adding «at» – ات –to the singular feminine or to the noun which has the feminine sign «ة» - «t».

There are other feminine signs or other words considered as feminine, but this is enough for the stage.

| **Recorded Exercise 18** | **تمـريـن مسجّل 18** |
|---|---|

أقْرأ

1 – زَرَعَ الفَلاّحُ الأرضَ.

2 – زَرَعَ الفَلاّحانِ الأرْضَ.

3 – زَرَعَ الفلاّحونَ الأرْضَ. (الفعل الماضي المعلوم)

4 – يَزْرَعُ الفلاّحُ الأرْضَ. (الفعل المضارع المعلوم)

5 – زُرِعَتِ الأَرْضُ. (الفعل الماضي المجهول)

6 – تُزْرَعُ الأَرْضُ. (الفعل المضارع المجهول)

7 – السَّماءُ صافِيَةٌ.

8 – أَحْمَدُ ذو مالْ.

9 – إشْتَرَى الرَّجُلُ كِتابَيْن.

10– أعْطى المعَلِّمُ النّاجحينَ جائزَةً.

## Unrecorded Exercise 19 تمرين غير مسجّل 19

■ أملأُ الفَراغَ بالكَلِمَةِ الصَّحيحَةِ **Fill in the blank with the correct word**

1 - يَصيدُ . . . . . . الطُّيورَ. (الصيادين - الصيادون)

2 - ساعَدَتْ . . . . . . . (المحتاجين - المحتاجون)

3 - جاء . . . . . مِنَ الخارج . (أخاه - أخوه)

4 - زُرْنا . . . . . . المَريضَ. (أخوه - أخاه)

5 - قرأ أحْمَدُ . . . . . . . (قِصَّتان - قصتَّيْن)

6 - السَّمَكُ في . . . . . . . (البحرُ - البحرِ)

7 - الكتابُ أَفْضَلُ . . . . . . . (صديق - صديقًا)

8 - أهَدينا . . . . . . هَدِيةً. (المعلماتَ - المعلماتِ)

9 - جاءَ الصَّديقُ . . . . . . . (باسمًا - باسمٌ)

10 - أُحِبُّ الفاكِهَةَ . . . . . . . (طازجةٌ - طازجةً)

---

hunt: يَصيد - birds: طيُور - needy: مُحْتاج، فقير

helped: سَاعدَ - abroad: الخارج - visit: يَزور - visited: زارَ

sick, ill: مَريض - better/best: أفْضَل / الأفْضلُ - present: يُهْدي

smiling: باسِم - fruit: فاكِهَة - fresh: طازَجَة

# 16 Demonstrative Nouns

# أسْمَــاءُ الإشـارَة 16

The demonstrative words in English are limited. They are «this, that, these, those». In Arabic they are far more than the English ones and more complicated.

For the beginners we will deal with this subject in a short and simple way. Here are some demonstrative nouns used for things, animals, or people:

1 - هَذا (used) تُسْتَعْمَل للإشارة إلى المفرْدَ المُذكّرِ القَريب .

هَذان (هَذين) للمُثنّى المذكَّر القَريب .

هؤُلاء للْجَمْع المذكر القَريب .

هَذه للمُفْرَد المؤنَّث القَريب .

هاتَان (هاتَيْن) للْمُثَنّى المُؤنَّث القَريب .

هؤلاء للجَمْع المؤنَّث القَريب .

2 - ذَاك (ذالك) لمُفْرَد غَيْر قريب - ذانكَ (ذَيْنك) لمثنّى غَيْر قريب .

أولئك (أولالك) لجَمْع مَذكَّر غَيْر قَريب .

تلْكَ لمُفْردَه مؤنَّثَة غَيْر قَريبه - تانِّك لمثنى مُؤنّث غَيْر قريب .

أَولُئك (أولا لك) لجمع مُؤنَّث غَير قَريب .

3- أسْمَاء إشارَةِ للمكان .

هُنا لِلْقريب - هُناكَ (هُنالِك) لِغَيْر القَريب .

مُلاحظة (**Note**) : كُلّ أسْماء الإشارة لا تَتَغيَّر حَرَكةُ آخر حَرْف فيـها ، إلاّ المثنّى فيكون بالألف والنُّون في حالةِ الرَّفْع وبالياءِ والنُّون في النَّصْب والجَرّ .

All the demonstrative nouns have fixed vowel sounds on the last letter **except** the dual which has (ān)-ان- in the subjective and(yn) -يْن- in the objective

## Recorded Exercise 20 — تمريـن مسجّل 20

فِي تِلْكَ السَّاعَةِ، وأنَا فِي هَذهِ الحالِ، شَعَرْتُ بِيَدٍ تَهُزّنِي هَزَّةً لَطيفةً. كانَتْ تِلْكَ اليدُ يَدَ صَديقي. أسْرَعَ قائلاً هَذا أنتَ! لِماذا تَجْلِسُ هُنا؟ تَعالَ نَدْخُلْ مَكْتَبَ المُديرِ هُناكَ. دَخَلْنا ذلِكَ المَكْتَبَ وسَلَّمْنا على المديرِ. طَلَبَ لَنا المُديرُ فِنْجانًا مِنَ القَهْوةِ العَرَبِيَّةِ اللّذيذةِ. شَرِبْنا هَذَيْنِ الفِنْجانَيْنِ وانْصَرَفْنا شاكِرَيْن.

## Unrecorded Exercise 21 — تمرين غير مسجّل 21

**Fill in the blank with the correct demonstrative:**

أضَعُ اسْمَ الإشارة المناسب في الفراغ التّالي :

1- . . . . . . الكتابُ مفيدٌ. (للقريب)

2- . . . . . . الزَّهْرَةُ جَميلةٌ. (للقريب)

3- . . . . . . الوَلَدُ يَلْعَبُ في الحَقْلِ. (لغير القريب).

4- . . . . . . البِنْتُ تَلْعَبُ بالكُرَةِ. (لغير القريب)

5- . . . . . . الأوْلادُ يَلْعَبونَ. (للقريب)

6- أعْطى المُعَلّمُ . . . . . . البِنْتَيْن جائزَتَيْن. (للقريب)

7- عَطَفْتُ على . . . . . . الفقيرَيْن. (للقريب)

8- . . . . . . البَناتُ يَجتَهِدْنَ في دروسِهِنَّ. (للقريب)

9- . . . . . . الملعبان واسعان. (للقريب)

# 17 «Kāna» - Verb To Be and Others كَــــــــــــانَ وأَخَــوَاتُهـــا

In Arabic, there are some verbs which have special function in the sentence.

These verbs are called:كان وأخواتها. they are many, but here we want to mention only **some** of them:

كانَ – صارَ – أَصْبَح – أَمْسى – ظَلَّ – باتَ – لَيْسَ .

They are called incomplete verbs: **أَفْعال ناقِصَة**

because they don't give complete meaning as other verbs.

When we say: شَرِبَ الولدُ, this gives meaning;

but when we say: . . . كانَ الطَّقْسُ, the meaning is incomplete.

When these verbs precede a sentence formed of two nouns, one subject and the other predicate, the subject الـمُبْتَدأ remains having «ḍammah» on its last letter, but the predicate - الخَبَـر - must have «Fatḥah» ـَ فَتْحَه or ـً فَتْحَتَين «Fatḥatayn» on its last letter.

The subject will be called «ẻsm kāna» -إسْم كان مَرْفوع

and the predicate will be called «khabar kāna» خَبَرْ كانَ مَنْصوب

**Example:**

1– الطَّقْسُ جَميلٌ – كان الطَّقْسُ جَميلاً 2– البَحْرُ عاصفٌ – لَيْسَ البَحرُ عاصِفًا .

**Example:** «be honest»: كُنْ أمينًا - In this example, the imperative verb: كُن functions as the past verb كانَ and as the present verb: يكونُ.

The subject of: «كُنْ - «إسم كُنْ»

is understood - (it is «you»: أنت) The predicate: «خَبر كُن»

is مَنْصوب «mansoub» - أمينًا -

**Notes**

**1**- «kana» كان may be complete, and then it froms with its subject a complete meaning and needs no «khabar».

**Example:** تَلاقي البَطَلان فكانَت المبارزةُ . كانَتْ = حَدَثَتْ

«The two heroes met and was the tournament».

Here «kanat» means happened: حَدَثَتْ and is complete in meaning The tournament المُبارَزةُ - is the doer of the action and not «esm» إسم كانَ

**2**- The predicate خبر of «kāna» may be a phrase, or a verb and other parts of speech.

**Example** of a phrase predicate: كان العُصْفورُ في القَفَصِ

**Example** of a verb predicate: كان الرَّجُلُ يَعْمَلُ في الحَقْلِ

نقول : «في القَفَص» في مَحَلِّ نصبْ خبَر كانَ .

ونقول: «يَعْمَل في الحقل» في مَحَلِّ نصبْ خبَرْ كانَ .

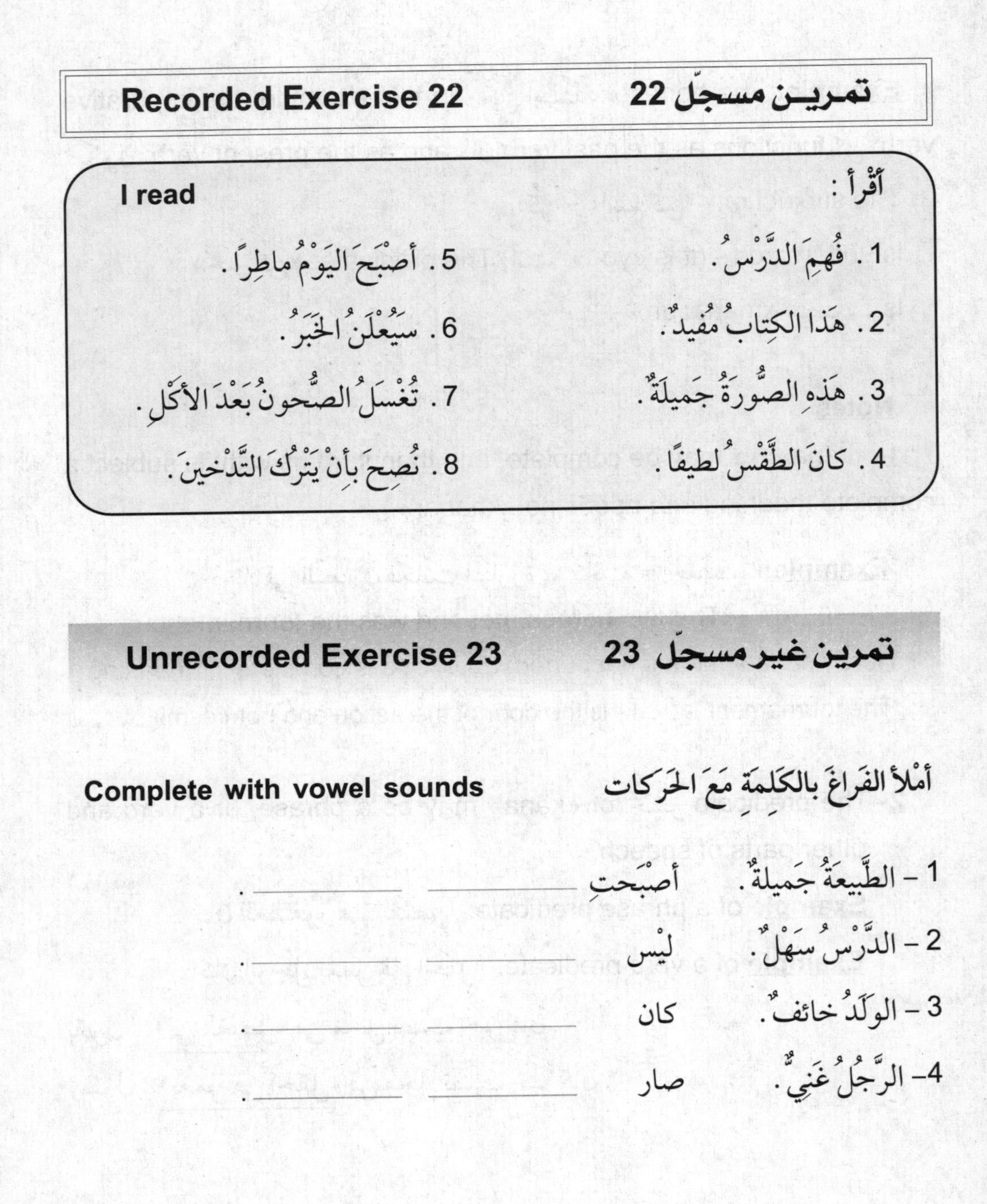

## Recorded Exercise 22 — تمرين مسجّل 22

**I read** — أقْرأ :

1. فُهِمَ الدَّرْسُ .
2. هَذا الكِتابُ مُفيدٌ .
3. هَذهِ الصُّورَةُ جَميلَةٌ .
4. كانَ الطَّقْسُ لطيفًا .
5. أصْبَحَ اليَوْمُ ماطِراً .
6. سَيُعْلَنُ الخَبَرُ .
7. تُغْسَلُ الصُّحونُ بَعْدَ الأكْلِ .
8. نُصِحَ بِأنْ يَتْرُكَ التَّدْخينَ .

## Unrecorded Exercise 23 — تمرين غير مسجّل 23

**Complete with vowel sounds** — أملأ الفراغ بالكَلمةِ مَعَ الحَركات

1 – الطَّبيعةُ جَميلةٌ .    أصْبَحتِ ________ ________ .

2 – الدَّرْسُ سَهْلٌ .    ليْس ________ ________ .

3 – الوَلَدُ خائفٌ .    كان ________ ________ .

4– الرَّجُلُ غَنِيٌّ .    صار ________ ________ .

# 18 «Ènna» and Others

# إن وأخـواتهـا 18

There are some articles, similar to verbs, called «ènna» and its sisters. They are similar to verbs in expressing some meanings as emphasizing and hoping ... etc. In the former chapter we discussed «kāna» and its sisters. Here, the function of these articles is a little different from that of «kāna» and its sisters.

These are the articles :

إنَّ – أنَّ – كأنَّ – لَكنَّ – لَيْتَ – لَعَلَّ

For emphasizing: إنَّ – أنَّ : لِلتَّأكيد

For comparison: كَأنَّ : لِلتَّشْبيه .

For giving different meaning from the former: لَكِنَّ

For wish (asking for something impossible): لَيْتَ

For hope (expecting some beloved events) لَعَلَّ

لِنأخذْ هذهِ الأمثلةَ على عملِ هَذه الحرُوفِ التّي تَسْبِقُ الـمُبْتَدأ والخَبَر :

1. ألوَقْتُ ثَمينٌ. أعْرفُ أنَّ الوَقْتَ ثَمينٌ.

2. زَيْدٌ شُجاعٌ. كَأنَّ زيْدًا أسَدٌ.

3. ألْبَيْتُ جَديدٌ. لَكِنَّ الأثَاثَ قَديمٌ.

4. ألْعَدْلُ مُطَبّقٌ. لَيْتَ العَدْلَ مطَبّقٌ.

---

justice عَدْل - time = وَقْت - precious = ثَمين - applied = مُطَبّق new = جَديد

furniture = أثَاث - old = قَديم

What did we notice in the examples? ماذا لاحظنا في الأمثلة السَّابقة؟

1- الاسْمُ الأوَّل وهُو المُبْتَدأ أصْبَحَ منصوبًا بالفَتْحة ويُسمَّى اسمَ هذه الأدوَات.

2- الاسْمُ الثَّاني وهُو الخَبر بَقِيَ مَرْفوعًا بالضَّمةِ ويُسَمَّى خبرَ هذهِ الأدوَات.

***We notice that:***

1- **The subject which has «o» on its last letter, had «a» when it became preceded by the articles and it will be called «ȇsm» of the article.**

2- **The predicate - the second noun - which has double «o» on its last letter, remained having the double «o» without change, and will be called «khabar» of the article.**

<u>**Notes**</u>

**1**- The predicate of these articles may be a phrase, a verbal sentence, or a noun sentence.

<u>**Example:**</u> (in the river: Predicate) إنّ القاربَ في النَّهْر.

<u>**Example:**</u> (is useful ....: Predicate) إنّ العلْمَ يَنْفَعُ الإنسانَ.

<u>**Example:**</u> (Its advantages ....: Predicate) إنّ الكَهْرباءَ فَوائدُها كَثيرةٌ.

نقول: شبْهُ الجُمْلَة «في النَّهْر» في مَحلّ رفْع خبَر إنَّ.

ونقول: «يَنْفعُ الإنْسَان» جملة فعْليَّة في مَحلّ رَفْع خَبَر إنَّ.

ونقول: «فَوائدُها كَثيرَة» جملة اسْمِيَّة مكوّنه من مُبْتَدأ ثانٍ وخبرُه، وهذه الجُمْلة في مَحلّ رَفْع خبَر إنّ.

---

boat : قارَب – in : في – river : نَهْر – knowledge : علْم

benefit : يَنْفَع – human - being : إنْسان – electricity : كَهْرَباء

benefits : فوائد – many : كثيرة

**2-** If the article «mā» - «ما» - is annexed to these articles, it will cancel their functions:

إنَّ الوَقْتَ ثَمينٌ تصبح : إنَّما الوَقْتُ ثَمينٌ .

ونقول «إنّ» بَطَلَ عَمَلُها . الوَقْتُ مُبْتَدأ مَرْفوع ، وليس إسْم إِنّ ، ثَمينٌ خَبَر المُبْتَدأ مَرْفوع ولَيْسَ خَبَر إِنّ .

**3 -** There are many cases where we say ẻnna إنَّ, not ẚnna أنَّ (Refer to Grammar books for details).

**4 - «lākenna» when pronounced «lāken» doesn't work on the subject and its predicate.**

يعني لكنَّ إذا خُفِّفَتْ إلى لكنْ يَبْطُل عَمَلُها :

مثال : البَيْتُ جَديدٌ لكنْ الأثاثُ قديمٌ . (لم تَعْمَلْ هنا)

## Unrecorded Exercise 24 — تمرين غير مسجّل 24

**Complete with the vowel sounds** — أَدْخِلِ الأدَواتِ التاليةَ معَ الحركات .

1 الطَّقْسُ جميلٌ. إنَّ ............ ............ .

2 الدَّواءُ نافِعٌ . لَعَلَّ ............ ............ .

3 الزَّهْرُ إكْليلٌ. كَأنَّ ............ ............ .

4 الغائِبُ قادمٌ. إنَّما ............ ............ .

5 البَحْرُ هادِئٌ. لَيْت ............ ............ .

# 19 «Ȃl Ḥāl» - Adverb of Manner الحـــــــال 19

## Adverb of Manner

Ȃl ḥāl **- adverb of manner in English - is used to express the state of a noun in the sentence** whether the noun concerned is in the subjective or in the objective case. **The noun referred to is called** صاحِبُ الحال in Arabic.

Usually صاحب الحال is مَعْرِفهَ i.e. either pronoun or noun with «the» - «ȃl» or proper noun - عَلَم - or the like.

**Example** : ذَهبَ الخـادِمُ مُسْـرِعًـا .

The servant wenty quickly.

**The word «the servant» is صاحب الحال and it is مَعْرِفه i.e. with «ألْ».**

**The word quickly مسرعًا expressed how was the verb done by the servant.**

صاحب الحال يكون مُشْتَقًا في الغالب .

What do we mean by مُشْتَّق? This Arabic word means that the adverb - ȃl ḥāl - is usually derived from a verb. The word «mosreȃ» is derived from the verb «ȃsraȃ».

**Notes: 1-** صاحب الحال **may be inflexible:** جامِد

**Example:** قرأتُ الكِتابَ بابًا بابًا .

Hereبابًا بابًا is حال. This حال is not derived from a verb, it is inflexible جامِد, but we can express it as flexible meaning «in details: مُفَصَّل»

The word مُفَصَّل is derived from the verb فَصَّل.

**2** -الحال must be «مَنْصوب»- manṣub - i.e. having <u>double a «fatḥatan»</u> (Refer to chapter 13 - II b)

**3** -الحال <u>usually</u> is نكِرَه versus to مَعْرِفه. Examples (smiling) بَاسِمًا .. (walking) مَاشِيًا . . . مُسْرِعًا . . .

Here the words:باسمًا، ماشيًا، مُسرِعًا are without «the» and such a noun without «The - ال» is called نَكِرَه in Arabic

**4** - يُمْكن أنْ يكونَ الحالُ كَلِمَة واحِدَة – مُفْرَد – أو جُمْلَه أو شبْه جُمْلَه .

**<u>Example:</u>** (ảl ḥāl is one word مُفْرَد) جاء الرَّجُلُ <u>ماشيًا</u> .

**<u>Example:</u>** رَأيْتُ الطِّفْلَ <u>وهُوَ يَضْحَكُ</u> .

وهُوَ يَضْحَكُ : جُمْلة في مَحَلْ نَصْب على الحال .

The sentence: <u>when he is laughing</u> functions as an adverb word «laughing».

**<u>Example</u>**: تكلّمَ الخَطيبُ فَوْقَ المِنْبرَ . (<u>فوق المنبر</u> : شِبْهُ جُمْلَه)

In the above sentence «<u>over the puplit</u>» represents a phrase fuctioning as an adverb word «standing».

---

child: طِفْل - talked: تَكَلّم - speaker, lecturer: خَطيب pulpit: منْبَر
assign: أُعَيّن - journey: رِحْلَة - impure: كَدِر - riding: راكِب - saw: شَاهَد، رأى
he: هُوَ - weep: يَبْكي

## Recorded Exercise 25 | تمرين مسجّل 25

I read | أقرأ

| | | |
|---|---|---|
| هُوَ يَمْشي | هُما يَمْشِيانِ | هُمْ يَمْشونَ |
| هي تَمْشي | هُما تَمْشِيانِ | هُنَّ يَمْشينَ |
| أنتَ تَمْشي | أَنْتُما تَمْشِيانِ | أَنْتُم تَمْشونَ |
| أَنْتِ تَمشينَ | أَنْتُما تَمْشِيانِ | أَنْتُنَّ تَمْشينَ |
| أنا أَمْشي | نَحْنُ نَمْشي | |

## Unrecorded Exercise 26 | تمرين غير مسجّل 26

I assign الحال and its reference | أُعَيِّنُ الحالَ وصاحِبَ الحال

| | صاحب الحال | الحال |
|---|---|---|
| 1. رَجَعَ أخوكَ منَ الرِّحْلَةِ ناجِحًا. | ______ | ______ |
| 2. لا تَشْرب الماءَ كَدِراً. | ______ | ______ |
| 3. جاء زَيْدٌ راكبًا. | ______ | ______ |
| 4. شاهَدْتُ العامِلَ يزْرُع الحَقْلَ. | ______ | ______ |
| 5. رأَيْتُ العُصْفورَ على الشَّجَرة. | ______ | ______ |
| 6. شاهَدتُ الطِّفْلَ وهُوَ يَبْكي. | ______ | ______ |

# 20 Almonādā - Vocative Case المُــــنَــــــادَى 20

**When we want to call a noun in Arabic,**

**this noun is called «مُنَادَى» monādā.**

The articles of calling are seven, the commonest ones are «yā»-يا, and «ây» - أَيْ

The called noun is two kinds: المُنادى يكون نُوْعَيْن :

1- One word: «mofrad» - مُفْرَد

2- «moḍāf» مُضاف (a noun added to another noun)

The one word «mofrad -مُفْرَد» is versus to «moḍaf - مُضاف» and includes «dual: مُثَّنى» and plural: جَمْع

**The noun in the vocative case** is considered a kind of object in the Arabic language. Therefore it must be manṣub: مَنْصوب vocally: لَفَظًا - or marfuâ- مَرْفوع - but locally should be «manṣub».

We express that state in Arabic as follows:

مَبْني على الضَمّ في مَحلّ نصَب

**I- The one word vocative: المفرد may be proper noun: مَعْرِفه, or intended noun without أل: نَـكِره .**

In this case it has «ḍammah»: ضمَّه as:

Yā Salimo, Yā Zaydo (proper nouns). يا سليمُ، يا زَيْدُ

and ya rajolo, ya walado (intended nouns without أل) . يا رَجُلُ، يا وَلَدُ

We say that the former nouns have ضَمّة but their place must be «manṣub: مَنْصوب

The same with: ya rajolan, ya momenun يا رَجُلان، يا مُؤْمنون

In former chapter, the dual has «an», and jamǎ ǎl moḍhakkar ǎl sā-lem has «un» in the subjective case, and when called they keep this sign, and we say in Arabic that they should be in the accusative case locally.

نَقُول بالعَرَبِيَّة أنّ «يا رَجُلُ» مَبْني على الضَمّ في مَحلّ نَصب لأنّه مُنادى ونَقُول أن «يا سليمُ» : مُنادى مَبْني على الضَمّ في مَحلّ نَصْب.

ونقول : «يا رجلان» : منادى مَبْني على الألف والنُّون لأنَّه مُثَنَّى في مَحلّ نَصْب.

ونقول : «يا مؤمنون» : منادى مَبْني على الواو والنُّون لأنَّه جَمْع مُذكَّر سالِم في مَحلّ نَصْب.

**II -** **المُنادى المُضاف أو النَّكِرَة غَيْر المَقْصودَة يكونُ منصوبًا.**

The called noun -المنادى - when added to another noun – المضاف – is in the accusative case – مَنصوب –

**Example:** يا عَبْدَ اللهِ ساعِدْني

- Here «aǎbd» is added to «ǎllah», therefore it must have «Faṭhah» on the last letter.

نقول بالعربية : عَبْدَ : مُنادى مُضاف مَنْصوب بالفَتْحَة.

- The unintended noun without «ǎl» – نكِرَة غَيْر مَقْصودَه must have «fathatan» on the last letter

**Example:** yā rajolan sāědni يا رَجُلاً ساعِدْني

We mean any man without specifying.

نَقول بالعَرَبِيَّة : رَجُلاً : مُنادى مَنْصوب بالفَتْحة لأنَّه نكِرَة غَيْر مَقْصودَه.

**III -** If we want to call a noun with «al» – معرفه– «بأل»

We add «ayyoha» أيُّها before the masculine

noun and «ảyyatohā» أيتّها before the Feminine noun
as follows: يا أيُّها الرَّجُلُ . . . . ، يا أيتَّها البِنْتُ

• Refer to the notes about the one word المفرد items I above for the vowel sound on the last letter of المنادى

## Recorded Exercise 27 — تمـريـن مسجّل 27

أقْرأ الجُملَ التَّالية مع الحركات

**I read the following sentences with the vowel sounds**

1. يا يُوسُفُ قُمْ بواجبكَ.
2. يا كَسْلانُ ادرُسْ.
3. يا شُعوبَ العالَمِ انبُذوا البَغضْاءَ.
4. يا مُحْسنُ ساعد الفُقَراءَ.
5. يا أيُّها الحُكّامُ اعْدلوا.
6. يا مُهاجِرونَ عُودوا إلى أوْطانِكُمْ.

## Recorded Exercise 28 — تمـريـن مسجّل 28

**I read** أقْـرأ

| | | |
|---|---|---|
| هُوَ يَعْلو | هُمَا يَعْلُوانِ | هُمْ يَعلُونَ |
| هيَ تَعلو | هُمَا تَعْلُوانِ | هُنَّ يَعلُونَ |
| أنتَ تَعْلو | أنْتما تَعلُوانِ | أنْتُم تَعلُونَ |
| أنتِ تَعْلينَ | أنْتُما تَعلُوانِ | أنْتُنَّ تَعلُونَ |
| أنا أَعْلو | نَحْنُ نَعْلو | |

---

do your duty: قُمْ بواجِبك - lazy: كَسْلان

peoples: شعُوب - world: العالَم - give up: انْبُذُوا - hatred: بَغْضاء

benevolent: مُحْسن - help: ساعد - the poor: الفُقَراء

rulers: حُكّام - be just: اَعْدلوا - immigrants: مُهاجرون

come back: ارجعوا، عودُوا - native countries: أوْطان

# 21 Relative Nouns — الأَسْمـاءُ المَوْصـولَة 21

What is the relative noun? — ما هُوَ الإسْمُ المَوْصول؟

الإسْمُ المَوْصولُ هُو الإسمُ الَّذي لايَتمُّ مَعْناه إلاّ بِجُمْلة بَعْدَه.

**The relative noun is the noun that is not complete by itself unless it is followed by a sentence.**

***Here are some relative nouns:***

الّذي – الّتي – اللّذان (اللّذيْن) – اللّتان (اللّتيْن)

اللّذين – اللّواتي (اللاّتي).

**Who** for persons. — مَن للعاقِل وهو مُشْتَرك للمُذكَّر والمؤنَّث.

and is common for masculine and Feminine.

**What** for things and is of common gender. — ما لِغَير العاقل.

**Who** for person - singular masculine. — الّذي : للعاقِل المذكَّر المفرَد.

**Who** for person - singular feminine. — الّتي : للعاقِلة المُؤنّثة المفرَدة.

**Who**/(m) - dual masculine - subj./and obj. — اللّذان/ اللّذيْن

**Who**/(m) - dual feminine - subj./and obj. — اللّتان/ اللّتيْن

**Who** plural masculine } for persons. { الّـذيـن

**Who** plural feminine } and things. { اللّواتي/ اللاّتي

**Note:** All the relative nouns have no vowel sounds – مَبْنيّه –

on the last letter, except the dual words اللّذان / اللّتان

These words have «ان» - «an» in the subjective case and «ين» - «yn» in the objective.

**Examples:** Respect your <u>parents</u> who educated you . إحتَرِمْ والدِيْك اللَّذَيْنَ ربَّياك .

- who: اللَّذَيْن - relative noun referring to <u>parents</u> which is dual masculine in the objective case: Therefore:

<u>اللَّذَيْن</u> : صفَة والدِيْك المَنْصوب ، وهو مَنْصوب بالياء والنُّون لأنَّه مُثَنَّى/ وهو مُذَكَّر .

This noun اللَّذَيْن agreed with its antecedent in case, number, and gender.

The same case with – اللَّتان –

The two girls whom you saw are polite. البِنْتان <u>اللَّتان</u> رأيتَهُما مُؤَدَّبتان .

The noun اللَّتان agreed with its antecedent - البنتان in case, number and gender

أَلبِنْتان مُثنَّى مُؤَنَّث مرْفوع بالألف والنُّون/ مُبْتَدأ .

نقول : «<u>اللَّتان</u>» نَعْت ، صِفَه ، البِنتَان مَرْفوع بالألِف والنُّون لأنَّه مُثنَّى/ وهُوَ مُؤَنَّث .

## Unrecorded Exercise 29     تمرين غير مسجّل 29

**أَضعُ الاسْمَ الموْصولَ المناسب**

**Fill in the blank with the correct relative noun**

1. اَلمرأةُ ...... تَهزُّ السَّريرَ بيَمينِها . تهزُّ العالَمَ بيَسارِها
2. ...... تزْرَعْ تَحْصُدْ .
3. هؤُلاء هُمْ ...... فازوا .
4. صَديقُك هُوَ ...... يُخْلِصُ لك .
5. ...... يَجتَهِد ينْجَحْ .
6. عاقَبَت المعلِّمَةُ الطَّالِباتِ ...... أهْمَلْنَ واجِبَهُنّ .
7. هَذان هُما الصَّديقانِ ...... زارَانا .
8. عَرَفْتُ البِنْتَين ...... نَالتَا الجائزَة .

---

woman: إمرأة - shake: يُهزّ - cradle: سَرير - right hand: يد يمين - left hand: يَد يَسار

sow: تَزْرَع - mow: تحصد - these: هؤُلاء - they: هُم - succeeded: فَازوا

be faithful: يُخْلص - study hard: يَجتَهد - punished: عاقَبَت - pupils: طالِبات -

neglected: أهْمَلْنَ - knew: عَرَف - received: نالَ

# Genetive Case — الإضـــــافـــــة

22

We have mentioned this case in articles 13/III. The first of the two nouns in the genetive case is called «ảl moḍāf».

The second noun is called «ảl moḍāf ẻlayhe». We mentioned that it has «e» on the last letter, and we say in Arabic ... الـمُضَاف إلَيهْ

المُضافُ إلَيْهِ مَجْرُورٌ بالكَسْرَةَ على آخرِه.

This case gives some meaning to المُضَاف .

Here are some rules about: المُضَاف .

1- المُضَافُ يَجِبُ أنْ لا يكونُ فيه تَنوينٌ ولا نونٌ.

ảl moḍāf must have neither «nun - ن» nor «tanwin» تنوين

**Examples:** We can't say: هَذانِ كتابان التَّاريخِ .

We say (without النون) هذان كتابا التّاريخِ .

We can't say قَرأْتُ كَتابًا التّاريخِ .

We say (without التَّنوين) قَرأْتُ كتابَ التاريخِ.

2- المُضاف يَجبُ أنَ يكونَ نكرة إذا أفادَتْ الإضافَةُ معنى التَّعريف أو التّخْصيص .

ảlmoḍāf must be without أل - i.e. نكِرَه if it is.

---

these: هذان + plural of this - history: تاريخ - read: يقرأ/ قَرأَ language:لُغَة

adding identification تعريف as كتابُ سَمير or

specification تخصيص as كتابُ لُغَة

Since Samir is a proper name, therefore, كتاب got identification تَعْريف, and لُغَة is نكره, there fore the word كتاب got what we call specification تَخْصيص.

It is wrong to say الكتابُ سَميرٍ / الكتابُ لُغَةٍ

## Recorded Exercise 30 تمرين مسجّل 30

I read أقْرأ

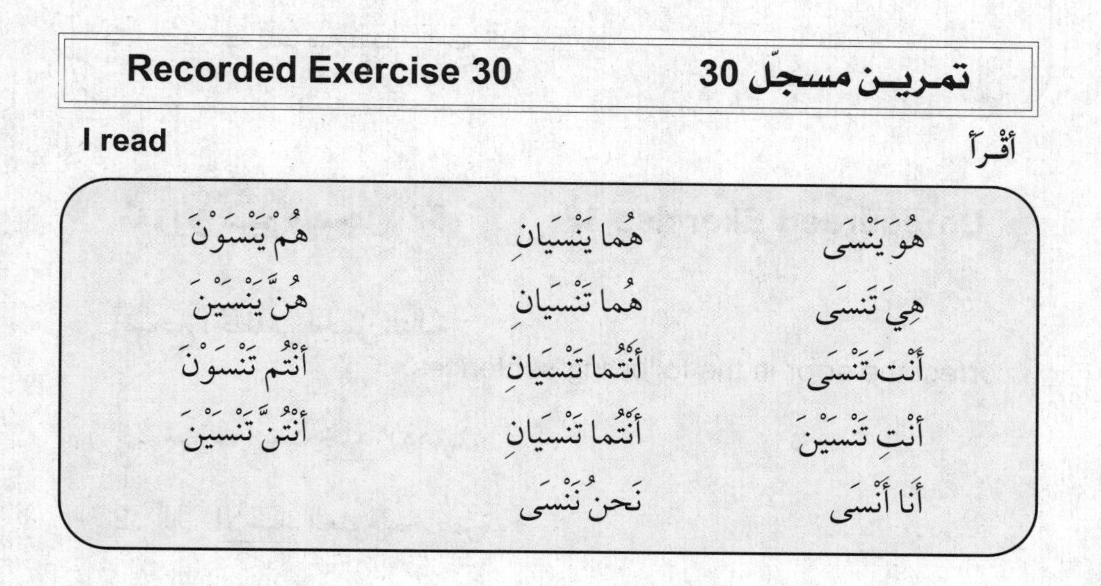

| | | |
|---|---|---|
| هُوَ يَنْسَى | هُما يَنْسَيانِ | هُمْ يَنْسَوْنَ |
| هِيَ تَنسَى | هُما تَنْسَيانِ | هُنَّ يَنْسَيْنَ |
| أنْتَ تَنْسَى | أنْتُما تَنْسَيانِ | أنْتُم تَنْسَوْنَ |
| أنْتِ تَنْسَيْنَ | أنْتُما تَنْسَيانِ | أنْتُنَّ تَنْسَيْنَ |
| أنا أنْسَى | نَحنُ نَنْسَى | |

---

built: بَنَى - minister: وَزير - factory: مَصْنَع - clothes: ألْبسَة

there are: تُوجَد - clouds: سُحُب - smoke: دُخان - library: مَكْتَبَة

references: مراجِع - many: عدَّة/ كَثير - times: مَرَّات

ring: خاتَمَ - gold: ذَهَبَ - delivered a lecture: ألقَى مُحاضَرَة

science: عُلوم - visited: زَارَ - member: عُضْو - parliament: بَرْلَمان

be: كُنْ - honest: أمينَ - honesty: أمَانَة - policy: سِياسَة

## Recorded Exercise 31 تمريـن مسجّل 31

أقْرأ الجُمَل التَّالية مَع الحَركات

I read the following sentences with the vowel sounds

1. بَنَى الوَزيرُ مَصْنعَ أَلْبِسَةٍ.
2. توُجَدُ سُحُبُ دُخان في المَدينَةِ.
3. مَكْتَبةُ المَدْرَسَةِ فيها مَراجعُ كَثيرةٌ.
4. قَرَأْتُ دَرْسَي التَّاريخِ عِدَّةَ مرّاتٍ.
5. مُعَلِّمو المَدْرَسة نَشيطونَ.

## Unrecorded Exercise 32 تمرين غير مسجّل 32

أصَحِّحُ الخطأ في الجُمَلِ التَّالِيَة:

I correct the error in the following sentences:

1. اشْتَرَت البِنْتُ خاتَمين ذَهَبٍ.
2. ألقَى الأستاذُ العلومِ مُحاضَرَةً.
3. زار عُضْوان البَرْلَمان رَوْضَةَ الأطْفالُ.
4. أصْبحَتْ شَوارِعُ القَرْيَةَ نَظيفَةٌ.
5. كُنْ أمينٌ، لأنَّ الأمانةُ أفْضَلُ سِياسةٍ.

# 23 Exception — الإسْتِثْناء 23

**1- What is exception?** — **1- ما هو الاستثناء**

Exception is the case of excepting a noun of a former statement. We say in English, for example, «all the students succeeded but - except- one».

We have the statement «all the students succeeded».

When we want to denote that one student did not succeed, we mean that one student is excepted - not included.

**مثال** : نقول بالعربية : نَجَحَ الطُّلابُ إلاَّ واحداً. معنى ذلك أن طالبًا واحدًا لم يَنْجَحْ – أي خَرَجَ مِن الحُكْم السَّابِق.

**2- What are the parts of exception?** — **2- ما هي أقسام - أرْكان- الاستثناء**

Its parts are the following: — أرْكانُه هي التَّالِية:

a- The noun excepted from: — أ- المُسْتَثْنَى منه

b- The excepted noun: — ب- المستثنى

c- The article of exception: — ج- أداةُ الاسْتِثْناء

| Examples: | | | |
|---|---|---|---|
| | = all the students - | مُسْتَثْنَى منه | الطّلابُ: |
| | = one | مُسْتَثْنَى | واحداً: |
| | = but | أداةُ الاسّتِثْناء | إلاّ |

---

succeeded: نَجَحَ - parts: أقْسام/ أرْكان - following: التَّالِية

Notes: **There are many exception articles, the most important is «ella»إلاَّ**

**There are also: «ghayr»:غَيْر - «sewā» سِوَى**

**«mā ảadā»: ما عدا ... and others**

3- ما هي حالاتُ الاسْمِ بَعْدَ إلاّ؟

**3- What are the cases of the noun after «ella»?**

أ- إذا كانَتِ الجمْلَةُ تامّةً ومُثْبَتَةً :

a- If the sentence is complete and affirmative - positive, in this case the noun must be «manṣub»

يَجب أنْ يكونَ الإِسْمُ في هذه الحالَةِ مَنصوباً .

Example: All the students passed except one.

نَجحَ الطُّلاَّبُ إلاّ واحِداً .

الطُّلاَّبُ: مستثنى منه مَذْكور، فالجُمْلَةُ تامَّةٌ .

**All the pupils «mostathna menho» mentioned. The sentence is complete.**

نَجَحَ الطلابُ: جُمْلَة مُثْبَتَه - غَيْر مَنْفِيَّه .

The pupils passed: positive sentence.

Therefore, the «mostathna» is manṣub» لِذَلِكَ: الـمُسْتَثْنى مَنْصوب: واحِداً

ب- إذا كانَتِ الجُمْلَةُ مَنْفيَّةً والمُسْتَثْنى منهُ مَذْكوراً/ النَّصبُ جائزٌ

**b- If the sentence is negative and «ảl mostathna menho is mentioned «ảnnaṣb» is not a must.**

**Example:** ما نَجحَ الطُّلاَّبُ إلاّ واحداً/ واحدٌ.

«wahedon» is in apposition to «toliabo» - «marfua».

ج- الجُمْلَة مَنْفيَّة والمُسْتَثْنَى مِنه غَيْر مَذْكور .المستثنى حَسَب مَوْقعه.

**c- The sentence is <u>negative</u>, and there is <u>no noun</u> before the exception article. In this case, the excepted noun after the article will be according to its function in the sentence.**

**Examples** : أمثلة : ما نَجَحَ إلاّ طَالِبٌ، طالبٌ: مستثنى مَرْفوع فاعل نجَحَ

«Ṭalebon» doer of the action of the verb نجح

ما اجْتَمَعْتُ إلاّ بسميرٍ. سَميرٍ: مُسْتَثْنَى مَجْرور بحَرْفِ الجرّ «ب».

«Samiren» - governed by the preposition «be».

لَم أَكْتُبْ إلاّ رِسَالةً. رسالةً: مستثنى مَنْصوب مَفْعول به للفِعْل أكتُبْ.

«resālatan» - object of the verb أكْتُبْ

**د- المستثنى بِغَيْر والأدوات الأخْرَى مثل «عدا» ، «سِوى» ، . . . .**

**There are other articles for exception as:**

«ghayr» غَيْر - «ʿādā» عدا - «sewā» سوى .... etc.

**Example:** أمثلة : نجح الطُّلابُ غيرَ واحدٍ غيرَ: مُسْتَثْنَى مَنْصوب.

واحد: مُضَاف إلَيْه مجرور

«ghayra» : mostathnā manṣub - «wāḥeden» moḍāf ʾelayhe majrur.

ما نَجَحَ غيرُ واحدٍ. غيرُ مستثنى فاعل نَجَحَ مَرْفوع،

واحدٍ مُضَاف إلَيْه مَجْرور

«ghayro»: doer of the action of the verb نجح

«waheden»: modaf elayhe majrur.

**What did we notice here?** ماذا لاحَظْنا هُنا؟

أ- حُكْمُ «غَيْر» والأدَوَات الأُخرى مثل حُكْمِ الاسْمِ بَعْدَ إلاَّ .

**a- The <u>rules</u> <u>concerning</u> the vowel sound on the last letter of «<u>ghayr</u>» and the <u>other articles</u> will be the <u>same</u> <u>as</u> the <u>noun</u> <u>after the article «ẽlla»</u>.**

ب- الاسْمُ بَعْدَ غَيْر والأدَواتِ الأُخْرى يكونُ مَجْروراً دائماً ، مُضَاف إليه .

**b- The noun after «ghayr» and the other articles will be «majrur» always - «moḍaf ẽlayhe».**

| Recorded Exercise 33 | تمريـن مسجّل 33 |
| --- | --- |

- هَذا المَريضُ الَّذي زُرْتُهُ صَديقي .
- هَذِهِ المَريضَةُ الَّتي أَزورُها جارَتي .
- هَذانِ المَريضانِ اللَّذانِ أَزورُهُما صَديقاي .
- هاتانِ المَريضَتانِ اللَّتانِ أَزورُهُما صَديقتاي .
- هَؤُلاءِ المَرْضَى الَّذينَ أَزورُهُمْ أَصْدِقائي .

---

do: يَعْمَل - duty: واجِب - generous: كَريم - stingy: بخيل

brave: شُجاع - defend: يُدافع عن - coward: جَبان - die: يَموت

exam: امْتِحان - punished: قاصَصَ - failure: فَشَل/ فاشِل

all: كُلّ/ جميع - invited: مَدْعُوّين - one: واحِد - apple: تُفَّاحَة

fail: يَفْشَل - call: نِداء

## Recorded Exercise 34 تمريـن مسجّل 34

I read the following with the vowel sounds: أقْرأ الجُملَ التّاليةَ معَ الحرَكات

1. يَعْمَلُ الإنْسانُ الواجبَ إلاّ الكَسُولَ.
2. يُساعِدُ الكَرِيمُ الفُقَراءَ إلاّ البَخيلَ.
3. يُدافِعُ الشُّجاعُ عَنِ الوَطنِ غيرَ الجَبانِ.
4. لَمْ يَمُتْ إلاّ الجبانُ.
5. ما نَجَحَ في الامْتِحانِ إلاّ المُجْتَهِدونَ.
6. ما قاصَصَ المعَلِّمُ إلاّ الفاشِلينَ.

## Unrecorded Exercise 35 تمرين غير مسجّل 35

Fill in the blank with the correct word : أملأ الفراغ بالكلمة الصحيحة

1. زارَني جَميعُ المدْعوّين إلاّ ......... (واحدٌ – واحدًا)
2. لم يَنْجَحْ.............. عليٍّ (غيرُ – غير)
3. لم يأكُلْ سَعيدٌ إلاّ ............ (تفّاحتان – تفاحتين)
4. لم يَفْشَلْ في الامْتِحان إلاّ......... (اثنين – اثنان)
5. ما جاء القَوْمُ إلاّ .............. (سليمٌ – سليمًا)
6. سَمِعَ الجَميعُ النّداءَ ....... واحدٍ. (غيرُ – غير)

## 24 Numbers الأعـــــــداد 24

| | | | |
|---|---|---|---|
| One | Wāḥed | واحِد | 1 |
| two | ễthnān | إثْنان | 2 |
| three | thalāthah | ثلاثَة | 3 |
| four | ẩrbaảah | أرْبَعة | 4 |
| five | khamsah | خَمْسَة | 5 |
| six | settah | سِتَّة | 6 |
| seven | sabảah | سَبْعَة | 7 |
| eight | thamaneyah | ثَمانية | 8 |
| nine | tesảah | تِسْعَة | 9 |
| ten | ảasharah | عَشَرة | 10 |
| eleven | ẩḥada ảashar | أحَد عشَر | 11 |
| twelve | ễthnā ảashar | إثْنَا عشَر | 12 |
| thirteen | thalathāhta ảashar | ثَلاثَة عشَر | 13 |
| fourteen | ẩrbaảta ảashar | أرْبَعَة عشَر | 14 |
| fifteen | khamsata ảashar | خَمْسَة عشَر | 15 |
| sixteen | settata ảashar | سِتَة عشَر | 16 |
| seventeen | sabảta ảashar | سَبْعَة عَشَر | 17 |
| eighteen | thamāneyata ảashar | ثَمَانِيَة عشَر | 18 |
| nineteen | tesảta ảashar | تِسْعَة عَشَر | 19 |
| twenty | ảeshrun | عشْرون | 20 |
| twenty one | wahed waảeshrun | واحد وعشْرون | 21 |
| twenty two | eathnan waaeshrun | إثْنَانَ وعشْرون | 22 |
| twenty three | thalathah waaeshrun | ثَلاثَة وعشْرون | 23 |

**Numbers are four categories:** الأعْداد أرْبَعَة أقْسام :

1- Singular numbers 1-10 — 1- الأعْداد المُفْرَدَة من 1-10

2- Compound numbers 11-19 — 2- الأعْداد المُرَكّبَة من 11-19

3- Decades 20-90 — 3- العُقود من 20-90

4- Joined numbers 21-99 — 4- المَعْطوف من 21-99

**1- a) We say one man, one girl** — 1- أ- نقول : رَجُلٌ واحدٌ/ بنْتٌ واحِدَةٌ

two men, two girls — رَجُلان اثْنانِ/ بِنْتانِ اثْنَتان

نلاحظ أن العَدَد من 1 - 2 يُطابِقَ المَعْدود في التَّذْكير والتَّأنيث .

**We notice that the numbers one-two agree with the counted noun - الإسم المعدود in gender. i.e. masculine with the counted masculine noun, feminine with the counted feminine noun.**

ونقول أحَدَ عَشَرَ واثنا عشَرَ رجلاً : مُذكّر مع المَعْدود المُذكَّر .

ونقول إحْدى عشْرَة واثْنتا عشْرَة بنتًا مُؤَنَّث مَع المَعْدود المؤنَّث .

ونقول واحِد وعِشْرونَ رَجُلاً واثْنان وعشْرُون رَجُلاً : مُذكَّر مَع المَعْدود المُذكَّر .

ونقول إحْدى وعِشْرون بِنْتًا واثْنتان وعِشْرون بنتًا : مُؤَنَّث مع المَعْدود المُؤَنَّث .

**We notice that: "ảḥadạ", "ẻthnā" are masculine with the counted masculine noun "rajol", and "ẻhdā", "ẻthnatā" are feminine with the counted feminine noun "bent". Also "åashara" with the masculine and "åashrata" with the feminine,**

**"wāḥed wa åeshrun" with the masculine "rajol",**

**"ẻḥdā wa åeshrun" with the feminine "bent".**

---

agree with: يُطابِق

ب- ونقول: ثَلاثَةُ رِجال وثَلاث بَناتٍ.

أرْبَعَة رِجالٍ وأرْبَعُ بنات.

عَشَرَةُ رِجالٍ وعَشْرُ بنات.

ماذا لاحظنا؟ العدد من 10-3 يؤنّث مَع المَعْدود المُذكَّر ويُذكَّر مع المَعْدود المُؤنَّث.

**b- What did we notice? The <u>number</u> from <u>3-10</u> is <u>feminine</u> "thalāthat" with the <u>counted</u> <u>masculine</u> "rējal", and <u>masculine</u> with the <u>counted</u> <u>feminine</u> "bānat". The same rule applies to numbers 4,5... till 10.**

ج- العدد مائة وألْف لا يَتَغيَّران أبدًا في جَميعِ الحالاتِ.

**c - The numbers <u>hundred</u>, and <u>thousand</u> never change in all cases. "meảh, ảlf", Keep the same form with masculine and feminine We say:**

مِائَةُ رَجُلٍ، مِائَةُ بِنْتٍ - أَلْفُ رَجُلٍ، أَلْفُ بِنْتٍ

without change: "meảt rajol, meảt bent" - "ảlf rajol, ảlf bent"... etc.

**2- Compound numbers.** 2 -ألأعداد المركبة.

نقول ثَلاثَة عشرَ رَجُلاً وثَلاثَ عشْرَةَ بنتًا،

ونقول أرْبَعةَ عشرَ رجُلاً وأرْبَعَ عشْرةَ بنتًا... (إلخ. etc)

What did we notice?

**The <u>numbers</u> from <u>3-9</u> compounded with "ten" are <u>masculine</u> with the counted feminine noun, and feminine with <u>counted masculine noun</u>.**

---

notice: يُلاحِظ - change: يتَغيّر - never: لا، أبَدًا - case: حَاله

**The word "ten" agrees with the counted noun after it.**

**3- Decades.** 3-العُقود

نقول عِشْرونَ رجلاً وعِشْرون بنْتًا ،

ونقول ثَلاثون رَجُلاً وثلاثونَ بنتًا . . . إلخ . . . etc) .

What did we notice? ماذا لاحظنا؟

**We notice that the numbers: 20, 30, ... etc.do not change. They have the same form with the counted nouns-masculine or feminine.**

**4- Joined numbers.** 4- الأعْداد المَعْطوفة .

حُكْمُ الأعْدادِ المَعْطوفه من 9 - 3 مِثْلُ حُكْمِ العَددِ المُفْرَدِ.

**The rule of the single numbers from 3-9 is the same as that of the single numbers of article one above mentioned, i.e. feminine with the counted masculine, and masculine with the counted feminine noun.**

مثال : خَمْسَةُ وعِشْرونَ رَجُلاً - خَمْسٌ وعِشْرون بنتًا . . . إلخ (etc) .

- **Notes: The compound numbers 11-19 keep the same vowel sounds on the last letter of each part, which is "a فَتْحه - except the number "ethnā aashar" where "ethna" is considered as "mothanna" - dual and has the same functional cases as "al mothannā".**
- **The noun after "hundred", "thousand", and "million" has two "ee" كَسْرَتَيْن on the last letter being "moḍāf elayhe" مُضَاف إلَيْه**

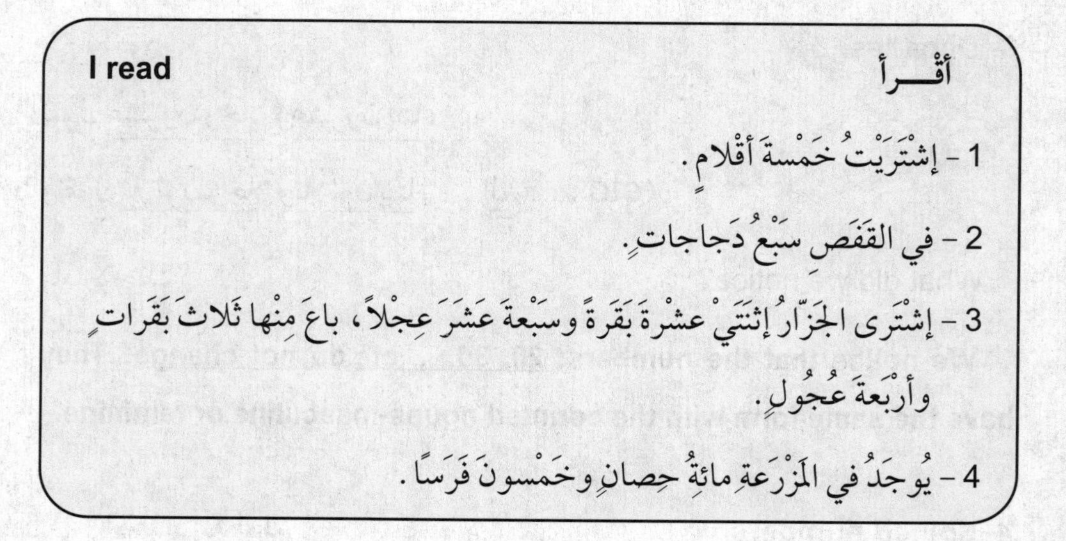

## Recorded Exercise 36 تمريـن مسجّل 36

**I read** أقْــرأ

1 - إشْتَرَيْتُ خَمْسَةَ أقْلامٍ .

2 - في القَفَصِ سَبْعُ دَجاجاتٍ.

3 - إشْتَرى الجَزّارُ إثْنَتَيْ عشْرةَ بَقَرةً وسَبْعةَ عَشَرَ عِجْلاً ، باعَ مِنْها ثَلاثَ بَقَراتٍ وأرْبَعةَ عُجُولٍ.

4 - يُوجَدُ في المَزْرَعةِ مائةُ حِصانٍ وخَمْسونَ فَرَساً .

---

cage: قَفَص, hens:دَجاجات, hen :دَجاجة,butcher: جَزّار,cow:بَقَرة, calf: عِجْل,sell:يَبيع

sold: باعَ, there is...are:يُوجَد,figure:رَقَم, figures:أرْقام, letter:حَرْف,

letters: حُروف, bag:مِحْفَظَة, bags:محفظات, graduated: تَخرّج, college:كُلّيّة

law: قانون , youth:شابّ, first: الأوَّل, second:الثّاني, magazine:مَجَلّة, ate:أكَلَ

egg: بَيْضَة, loaf:رَغيف

## Unrecorded Exercise 37 — تمرين غير مسجّل 37

I write the figures in letters: — أكتب الأرقام بالحروف :

1 - إشْتَرَى الولدُ 9 كُتُبٍ ..........................................

2 - باع الرَّجُلُ 4 مَحْفَظاتٍ ..........................................

3 - تَخرّجَ مِنْ كُلِيَّةِ الحُقوقِ 15 فتاةً (بنتًا)..........................................

و16 شابًا..........................................

4 - يُوجَدُ في المدرسةِ 10 صُفوفٍ..........................................

في الصَّفِ الأوَّلِ 25 ولدًا..........................................

وفي الصَّفِ الثاني 21 بنتًا..........................................

5 - في مكْتَبَتي 1000 كتابٍ و100 مجلّةٍ ..........................................

6 - أكَلَ الرَّجُلُ بيضَتَيْنِ 2 ورغيفًا 1 .................. و ..................

# 25 Ordinal Numbers — الأعْدادُ التَّرْتيبِيَّة 25

| | | |
|---|---|---|
| The first | a̓l a̓wwal | الأوَّل |
| The second | a̓ththāni | الثّاني |
| The third | a̓ththāleth | الثّالث |
| The fourth | a̓rrābea̔ | الرّابِع |
| The fifth | a̓l khāmes | الخامَس |
| The sixth | a̓ssādes | السّادِس |
| The seventh | a̓ssābea̔ | السّابِع |
| The eighth | a̓ththāmen | الثّامِن |
| The nineth | a̓ttāsea̔ | التّاسِع |
| The tenth | a̓la̔āsher | العاشِر |
| The eleventh | a̓lḥādi a̔ashar | الحادي عَشْر |
| The twelfth | a̓ththāni a̔ashar | الثاني عَشْر |
| The thirteenth | a̓ththāleth a̔ashar | الثالِث عَشْر |
| | | ........ |
| | | ........ |
| The twentieth | a̓l a̔eshrun | العِشْرون |
| The twentieth first | a̓l wāḥed wala̔eshrun | الواحِد والعِشْرون |
| The twentieth second | a̓ththāni wala̔eshrun | الثاني والعِشْرون |

| | | |
|---|---|---|
| The twentieth third | ȧththāleth walȧeshrun | الثالِث والعِشْرون |
| | | ........ |
| | | ........ |
| The thirtieth | ȧththalāthun | الثَّلاثون |
| The fortieth | ȧlȧrbaȧun | الأرْبَعون |
| The fiftieth | ȧl khamsun | الخَمْسُون |
| The sixtieth | ȧssettun | السِّتّون |
| The seventieth | ȧssabȧun | السَّبْعون |
| The eightieth | ȧththamānun | الثَّمانون |
| The ninetieth | ȧttesȧun | التِّسْعون |
| The hundredth | ȧlmeȧh | المائَة |
| The thousandth | ȧlȧlf | الأَلْف |
| The millionth | ȧlmalyun | المَلْيون |

## Recorded Exercise 38 — تمـريـن مسجّل 38

I read — أقْـرأ

أَلْوَلَدُ الأوَّلُ في الصَّفّْ. — أَلشَّهرُ التَّاسعُ.

ألبِنْتُ الأُولَى في الصَّفّْ. — أَليَوْمُ الرَّابعُ والعِشْرونْ.

أَلفَصْلُ الثَّاني. — أَلمَقعَدُ الخامِسَ عَشَرَ.

أَلسَّنَةُ الثَّالِثَةُ. — أَلغُرْفَةُ السَّادسِةَ عَشْرَةَ.

1 - العددُ التَّرتيبي يَدُلّ على تَرْتيبِ المَعْدودِ بالنّسبةِ لغَيْره .

**1- The Ordinal number denotes the arrangement of the counted number in proportion to others.**

Example: He is the sixth in the class. **مثال :** هُوَ السّادِسُ في الصّفِ .

2- **العدد الترّتيبي المُفرَد المُركّب يُذكّر معَ المُذكّر ويُؤنّث معَ المُؤنّث .**

**2- The ordinal number - singular and compound - is masculine with the counted masculine noun, and feminine with the counted feminine noun.**

**Example:** The fifth class. «ȧṣṣaf ȧl khāmes». **مثال :** الصَّفُّ الخامِسُ .

(العدد) الخامِسُ مذكّر لأن الصَّفَّ (المعدود) مُذكّر .

**Example:** The fifth year. ȧssanah ȧlkhāmesah **مثال :** السَّنَةُ الخامِسَةُ .

العدد : الخامِسةُ مُؤنّث – المعدود : السَّنَة مُؤنّث .

**Example:** The fifteenth lesson «ȧddars ȧl khāmes ȧashar» . **مثال :** الدَّرْسُ الخامسَ عَشَرَ .

العدد : الخامِسَ عَشرَ مُذكَّر – المعدود : الدّرس مُذكّر .

**Example**: aṣṣafḥah ȧlkhāmesah ȧashrah . **مثال :** الصَّفْحَةُ الخامسةَ عشْرةَ .

العدد : الخامِسَةَ عشْرةَ مؤنَّث – المعدود : الصفحة مُؤنّث .

---

denote: يَدُلّ علىَ - arrangement: تَرْتيب - in proportion to : بالنّسبه ل -

others: غَيْرهم ، الأخَرين

3- المَعْطوف: يُذْكَّرُ الجُزْءُ الأوَّلُ فقَطْ معَ المُذكَّر ويُؤَنَّث معَ المؤَنَّث وتَبْقَى العُقودُ بِدونِ تَغْيير.

**3- The joined number: The first part of it is <u>masculine</u> <u>with the</u> <u>counted masculine</u>, and <u>feminine</u> <u>with the</u> <u>counted feminine</u> noun. The decades: 20, 30... etc remain the same without changes.**

مثال : الوَلَدُ الخامِسُ والعِشْرون . البِنْتُ الخامِسَةُ والعِشْرون .

الخامِسُ مُذَكَّر معَ المَعْدُود المُذكَّر ، الخَامِسَةُ مؤَنَّث معَ المَعْدود المؤَنَّث .

العِشْرون لم تَتَغَيَّرْ .

4- مائةِ وألفْ يَبْقَيان بِلَفْظ واحدٍ مَع المُذكَّر والمُؤَنَّث .

مثال : المَقْعَد المائةُ : الطَّاوِلَةُ المائَةُ - العامُ الألْفُ . السَّنَةُ الألْفُ .

**4- The numbers: «ȃl meȃh», «ȃl ȃlf» remain unchanged with the masculine words «maqȃad, ȃȃm», and with the feminine words «ȃṭṭāwelah», «ȃssanah».**

---

change: تَغْيير - table: طاوِلَة - year: عام/ سَنة

## Recorded Exercise 39 تمريـن مسجّل 39

**أقْرأ** **I read**

في الحَديقَةِ ثَلاثونَ صَفًا مِنَ الأَشْجارِ. في الصَّفِّ الأوَّل عَشَرُ أَشْجارٍ وَفي الصَّفِّ الثّاني أَرْبَعَ عَشْرَةَ شَجَرَةً، وفي الصَّفِّ الخَامِسِ سَبْعَ عَشْرَةَ شَجَرَةً، وفي الصَّفِّ الثّامِنَ عَشَرَ إثْنَتانِ وعِشْرونَ شَجَرةً، وفي الصَّفِّ التاسِعَ عشرَ خَمْسَ عَشْرَةَ شَجَرَةً، وفي الصَّفِّ العِشْرينَ ثلاثٌ وعِشْرونَ شَجرةً.

## Unrecorded Exercise 40 تمرين غير مسجّل 40

**I write the Figures With vowel sounds** : أكْتُبُ الأرْقام بالحُروف معَ الحَركات

1. قَرأْتُ الدَّرْسَ ال 13.
2. كَتَبْتُ الصَّفْحةَ ال 51.
3. قَرأْتُ المقالةَ ال 8.
4. أنا في العام ال 14 مِنْ عُمْري.
5. أخْتي في السَّنة ال 20 مِنِ عُمْرِها.
6. أخي في العام أل 45 من عمرِه.
7. الصَّفْحةُ ال 100.
8. العامُ ال 1000.

---

page:صَفْحَة - essay:مَقالَه - I: أنا - sister:أخْت

of age:مِنَ العُمْر، مِن عُمْري، مِنْ عُمْرِها. . . .

## 26 Days — الأيّام

| | | |
|---|---|---|
| The Days | ảlảyyām | الأيّام |
| Monday | ảlethnayn | الاثّنين |
| Tuesday | ảththolathā | الثلاثاء |
| Wednesday | ảl ảrbeảā | الأرْبعاء |
| Thursday | ảl khamis | الخَميس |
| Friday | ảl jomảah | الجُمْعَة |
| Saturday | ảssabt | السَّبْت |
| Sunday | ảl ảḥad | الأحَد |

## 27 Months — الأشهر

| | | |
|---|---|---|
| The Months | ảl ảshhor | الأشْهُر |
| January | Kānun ảththāni | كانون الثّاني |
| February | Shobāṭ | شُباط |
| March | ảdhār | آذار |
| April | nisān | نيسان |
| May | ảyyār | أيّار |
| June | ḥozayrān | حُزَيْران |

| | | |
|---|---|---|
| July | tammuz | تمّوز |
| August | ả̄b | آب |
| September | ảylul | أيْلول |
| October | tashrin ảl ảwwal | تَشْرين الأوّل |
| November | tashrin ảththāni | تَشْرين الثّاني |
| December | kānun ảl ảẃwal | كانون الأوّل |

## 28 Seasons — الفُصول

| | | |
|---|---|---|
| The seasons | alfoṣul | الفُصول |
| Season | faṣl | فَصْل |
| Winter | ảshshetā' | الشّتاء |
| Spring | ảrrabiả | الرَّبيع |
| Summer | ảṣṣayf | الصَّيْف |
| Autumn | ảl kharif | الخَريف |

# 29 Expressing Time

# 29 التعبير عن الوقت

| | | |
|---|---|---|
| Expressing time | ẚttaẚbir ẚane lwaqt | التَّعْبير عَنْ الوَقْت |
| hour | sāẚah | ساعة |
| minute | daqiqah | دَقيقَة |
| Second | thāneyah | ثانيَة |
| day | yawm | يَوْم |
| week | ởsbuẚ | أسْبُوع |
| month | shahr | شَهْر |
| year | sanah | سَنَة |
| daytime | nahār | نَهار |
| night | layl | لَيْل |
| mid-day | montaṣaf ảnnahār | مُنْتَصَف النَّهار |
| yesterday | ảlbāreḥah, ảmse | البارحة، أمسِ |
| daily | yawmeii | يَوْمِيّ |
| weekly | ởsbuẚii | أسبُوعِيّ |
| yearly | sanawii | سَنَوِيّ |
| good morning | ṣabāḥ ảl khayr | صَبَاحُ الخَير |
| good afternoon/good evening | masāɔ ảl khayr | مَساءُ الخَيْر |
| good night | toṣbeḥ ẚlā khayr | تُصْبح على خَيْر |
| half an hour | neṣf sāẚah | نِصفَ ساعَه |

| | | |
|---|---|---|
| quarter of an hour | roba̔ sāa̔h | رُبْع ساعَه |
| five o'clock | a̓ssāa̔h a̓l kha̔mesah | السَّاعَة الخامِسه |
| ten to five | a̓l khāmesah e̓lla a̔ashrah | الخامِسَةُ إلاّ عشْره |
| ten past five | a̓l khāmesah wa a̔ashrah | الخامِسَه وعَشْره |
| half past five | a̓l khāmesah wanneṣf | الخامِسَه والنِّصْف |
| twenty past five | a̓l khāmesah waththolth | الخامِسَه والثُّلْث |
| quarter past five | a̓l khāmesah warroba̔ | الخامِسَه والرُّبْع |
| in the morning | fi ṣṣabāḥ, ṣabāḥan | في الصَّباح ، صباحًا |
| at noon | ḍhohran | ظُهْرًا |
| in the afternoon | baa̔da ḍhḍhohr | بَعْدَ الظُّهْر |
| at night | laylan | ليلاً |
| in the evening | fil masāↄ | في المَساء |

مِنْ فَضْلِك ، كَمِ السَّاعةُ الآن؟

Please, what time is it now?

now : الآن                                        Please : مِنْ فَضْلك

<u>What</u> time is it?                                        كَمِ السَّاعَةُ/ ما السَّاعةُ : ؟

Time: a̓ssāa̔h

It is six o'clock <u>exactly</u>.                                        الّساعةُ السّادِسَةُ <u>تَمامًا</u>

Exactly: tamaman

## Unrecorded Exercise 41     تمرين غير مسجّل 41

I write the following in Arabic     أكتُب ما يلي بالعربية

1. It is five o'clock. - 1

2. It is half past seven. - 2

3. It is five to ten. - 3

4. Good night. - 4

5. It is quarter past six - 5

6. Good evening - 6

7. Good morning - 7

# 30 Weather — الطَّقْس

| | | |
|---|---|---|
| The Weather | ảṭṭaqs | الطَّقْس |
| wind - winds | riḥ–reyāḥ | رِيح – رِياح |
| air | hawāↄ | هواء |
| snow | thalj | ثَلْج |
| cold | bāred | بارِد |
| hot | ḥārr | حَارّ |
| fine | laṭif | لَطيف |
| stormy | ảāṣef | عاصِف |
| rainy | māṭer | ماطِر |
| how | kayfa | كَيْفَ |

How is the weather today? — كيف الطَّقْسُ اليوم؟

It is a rainy day. — إنه يَوْمٌ مـاطِر.

It will be fine tomorrow. — سَيكونُ الطقسُ لَطيفًا غدًا.

It was a very cold night. — كانَتْ لَيْلَةً باردة جداً.

---

today:اليَوْم – night:لَيْل / لَيْلَة - will: س/ سَوْف - tomorrow: غَدًا - was:كان - very: جِداً

were: كان with the 2nd person, and with the 3rd person plural.

was:كان with the 1st person singular, and the 3rd person singular.

fall, fell: يَسْقُط ، سقط - moutain/s: جبَل/ جِبال

The winds were strong. وكـانَتْ الرِّياحُ قَوِيّة .

The snow fell on the mountains. سَقطَ الثَّلْجُ على الجِبال .

today: ảlyawm - will be: sayakun

tomorrow: ghadan - was: kāna(t) - very: jeddan

were: kanū - konta - konte - (see foot- note page 90).

fall: yasqoṭ - fell: saqaṭa - mountain: jabal.

mountains: jebāl.

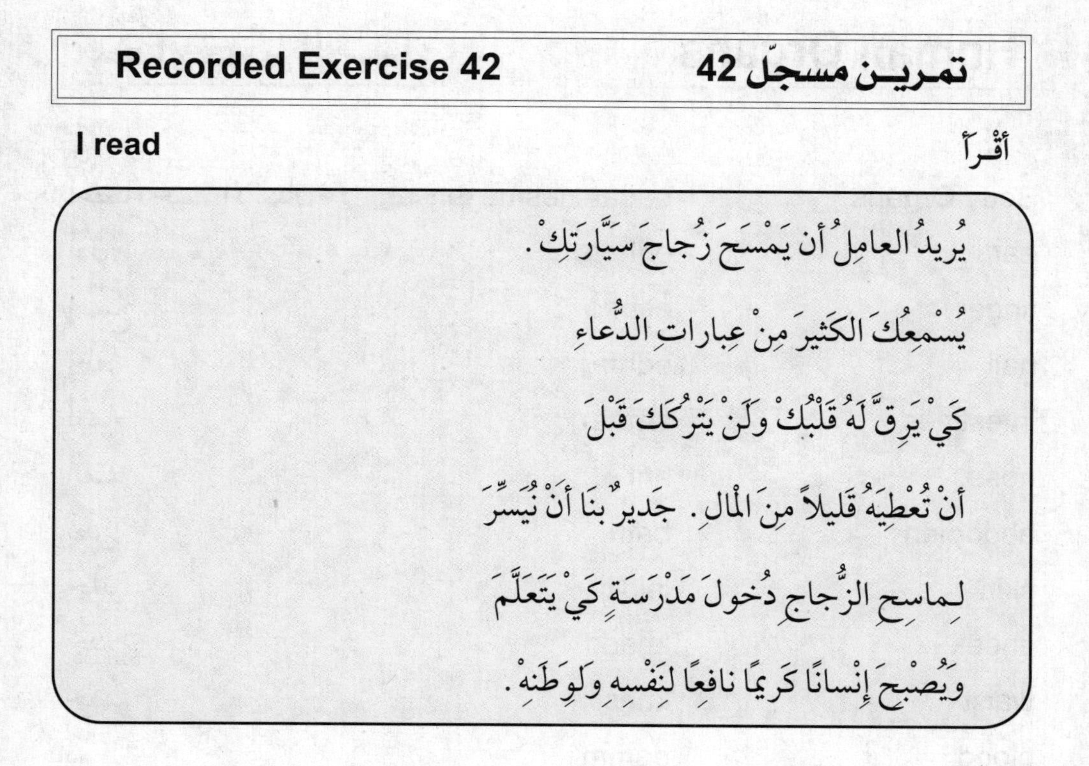

## Recorded Exercise 42 تمـريـن مسجّل 42

**I read** أقْـرأ

يُريدُ العامِلُ أن يَمْسَحَ زُجاجَ سيَّارَتِكْ .

يُسْمِعُكَ الكَثيرَ مِنْ عِباراتِ الدُّعاءِ

كَي يَرِقَّ لَهُ قَلْبُكْ ولَنْ يَتْرُكَكَ قَبْلَ

أنْ تُعْطِيَهُ قَليلاً مِنَ المْالِ. جَديرٌ بِنا أنْ نُيَسِّرَ

لِماسِحِ الزُّجاجِ دُخولَ مَدْرَسَةٍ كَي يَتَعَلَّمَ

ويُصْبِحَ إِنْسانًا كَريمًا نافِعًا لِنَفْسِهِ ولِوَطَنِهْ .

## 31 Senses — الحَــــــواسّ

| | | |
|---|---|---|
| The Senses | ̉alḥawāss | الحَواسّ |
| taste | ̉adhdhawq | الذَّوْق |
| hearing | ̉assamȁ | السَّمْع |
| smell | ̉ashshamm | الشَّمّ |
| touch | ̉allams | اللَّمْس |
| sight | ̉annaḍhar | النَّظَر |

## 32 Human Organs — أعْضَاء جِسْمِ الإنْسان

| | | |
|---|---|---|
| Body Organs | ̉aȁḍā̉ , j̉esme ̉ıensān | أعضاء جسم الإنسان |
| ear | ̉odhon | أذُن |
| finger | ̉eṣbaȁ | إصبَع |
| nail | ̉eḍhfar | إظْفَر |
| intestines | ̉amȁa̓ | أمْعاء |
| nose | ̉anf | أنْف |
| abdomen | baṭn | بَطْن |
| skin | jeld | جِلْد |
| cheek | khadd | خَدّ |
| waist | khaṣr | خَصْر |
| blood | damm | دَمّ |
| brain | demāgh | دِماغ |
| chin | dhaqn | ذقْن |
| head | raȁs | رَأس |
| lung | reȁh | رِئَة |

| | | |
|---|---|---|
| leg | rejl | رِجْل |
| tooth | senn | سِنّ |
| moustache | shāreb | شارب |
| lip | shafah | شَفَه |
| artery | sheryān | شِريَان |
| hair | shaa̔r | شَعْر |
| chest- breast | ṣadr | صَدْر |
| back | ḍhahr | ظَهْر |
| bone | a̔aḍhm | عَظْم |
| neck | a̔onoq | عُنُق |
| eye | a̔ayn | عَيْن |
| mouth | famm | فَم |
| foot | qadam | قَدَم |
| heart | qalb | قَلْب |
| liver | kabed | كَبِد |
| shoulder | katef | كَتِف |
| kidney | kelyah | كِلْيَه |
| beard | leḥyah | لِحْيَه |
| flesh | laḥm | لَحْم |
| tongue | lesān | لِسان |
| stomach | maa̔edah | مَعِده |
| face | wajh | وَجْه |
| hip | werk | ورْك |
| hand | yad | يَد |

brow: حاجب ḥājeb

# 33 Colours

# 33 الألْـــــــوان

| | | |
|---|---|---|
| Colours | ả̉l ả̉lwān | الألوان |
| white | ả̉byaḍ | أبْيَض |
| red | ả̉ḥmar | أحْمَر |
| green | ả̉khḍar | أخْضَر |
| blue | ả̉zraq | أزْرَق |
| brunet | ả̉smar | أسْمَر |
| black | ả̉swad | أسْوَد |
| blond | ả̉shqar | أشْقَر |
| yellow | ả̉ṣfar | أصْفَر |
| orange | bortoqāli | بُرْتُقَالي |
| brown | benni | بِنّي |
| pink | zahri | زَهْري |
| reddish brown | kastanā̉ei | كَسْتَنائي |
| light | fāteḥ | فاتِح |
| dark | ghāmeq | غامِق |

# Adjectives

# الـــصِّـــفـــات



| | | |
|---|---|---|
| Adjectives | åṣṣefāt | الصِّفات |
| cheap | rakhiṣ | رَخيص |
| expensive | ghāli | غالي |
| clean | naḍhif | نَظيف |
| dirty | wasekh | وَسِخ |
| easy | sahl | سَهْل |
| difficult | ṣaåb | صَعْب |
| wide-broad | åariḍ | عَريض |
| narrow-tight | ḍayyeq | ضَيِّق |
| loose | wāseå | واسِع |
| strong | qawii | قَوِيّ |
| weak | ḍaåif | ضَعيف |
| big | kabir | كَبير |
| small- young | ṣaghir | صَغير |
| beautiful | jamil | جَميل |
| ugly | qabiḥ | قَبيح |
| new | jadid | جَديد |
| old | qadim - kabir åssen | قَديم-كَبيرُ السِّنّ |
| tall | ṭawil | طَويل |
| short | qaṣir | قَصير |
| high | åālen | عالٍ |
| low | monkhafeḍ | مُنْخفِض |

# 35 Family and Relatives

# 35 العائِلة والأقارِب

| Family and Relatives | ảla̔ảelah walảqāreb | العائِلة والأقارِب |
|---|---|---|
| father | ảbb | أب |
| mother | ỏmm | أُمّ |
| son | ẻbn | إبْن |
| daughter | ẻbnah | إبْنَة |
| boy | walad | وَلَد |
| girl | bent | بِنْت |
| brother | ảkh | أَخ |
| sister | ỏkht | أُخْت |
| grand-father | jadd | جَدّ |
| grand-mother | jaddah | جَدَّه |
| uncle | khāl | خَال |
| aunt | khālah | خَالَه |
| uncle | a̔amm | عَمّ |
| aunt | a̔ammah | عَمَّه |
| nephew | ẻbne lảkh, elỏkht | إبْنِ الأخ/ الأخْت |
| niece | ẻbnate lảkh, elỏkht | إبْنَةِ الأخ/ الأخْتِ |
| cousin | ẻbne la̔amm | إبْنِ العَمّ |
| cousin | ẻbnate la̔amm | إبْنَةِ العَمّ |

| | | |
|---|---|---|
| cousin | ẻbne lkhāl | إبْنِ الخَال |
| cousin | ẻbnate lkhāl | إبْنَةِ الخَال |
| son-in-law | ṣehr | صِهْر |
| daughter-in-law | kennah | كِنّه (زَوْجة الإبن) |
| father-in-law | ȃamm | أبُ الزَّوْج/ الزَّوْجَة (عمّ) |
| mother-in-law | ḥamāh | أمُّ الزَّوج/ الزَّوْجَة (حماه) |
| sister-in-law | ỏkhtezzawj, zawjah | أخْتُ الزَّوْج/ الزَّوْجَة |
| brother-in-law | ảkho zzawj, zzawjah | أخُ الزَّوج، الزَّوْجة |

- تَتَألَّف عائِلتي مِنْ أربْعَة أشْخَاص . tataȃllaf ȃȃelati men ảrbaȃat ashkhāṣ.

My family consists of four individuals.

- عِنْدي وَلَدٌ وبنْتٌ . ȃendi walad wa bent.

I have one son and one daughter.

- أنَا أحِبُّ أقَاربي وهُمْ يُحِبُّونَني . ảnā ỏḥebbo ảqārebi wa hom yoḥebbunani.

I love my relatives and they love me.

- أنَا أزورُهـم وهُـمْ يَزورونَـني . ảnā ảzurohom wa hom yazurunani

I visit them and they visit me.

# 36 At the Airport

# في المطـــار 36

At The Airport | fil maṭār | في المطار

sa ȏsāfer jawwan ȇlā... سأسافِر جوّاً إلى . . .

I will travel by air to...

hādhehi heya ḥaqāȇbi. هَذِه هيَ حَقَائبي .

This is my baggage.

ȏrido ȃn ȃstalemaha honāk. أريدُ أنْ أستَلمِها هُناك.

I want to get it there.

lakal ḥaqq be hadhāl wazne faqaṭ. لَكَ الحق ّ بِهذا الوَزْن فَقَطْ .

You are allowed to carry this weight only.

matā satoqleȃo ṭṭāȇrah? مَتَى ستُقلِعُ الطَّائِرَة؟

When will the plane take off?

mā raqam bawwabatel ȃobur? ما رقَمُ بوَّابَة العُبور؟

What is the gate number?

matā naṣel? مَتَى نَصِل؟

When will we arrive?

men ȃyna ȃnta qādem? مِنْ أيْن أنتَ قادِم؟

Where are you coming from?

ȃyna maktabol ȇsteȃlāmāt? أينَ مكتَبُ الإستِعْلامات؟

Where is the information office?

jawāz safarek men faḍlek. جَوازْ سَفَرِكْ، مِنْ فَضْلك .

Your passport, please.

hal maɛak shayʾ mamnuɛ? هَلْ مَعَكْ شَيْء مَمْنوع؟

Do you have any forbidden thing?

lā, maɛi baɛḍol hadāyā lelaʾṣdeqāʾ. لا ، مَعي بَعْضُ الهَدايا للأصْدِقاء .

No, I have some gifts for my friends.

sallamto ʾamteɛati lelḥammal leyazenahā. سَلَّمْتُ أَمْتِعَتي للحَمّال لِيَزنَها .

I have given my baggage to the porter to weigh it.

# 37 At the Customs — في الجمارك 37

| | | |
|---|---|---|
| At The Customs | fil jamārek | في الجمارك |
| customs official | mowaḍhḍhafo l jomrok | مُوَظّفُ الجُمْرُك |
| luggage | ảmteảah | أمْتِعَة |
| bags | ḥaqāeb | حَقائِب |
| passport | jawāz safar | جَواز سَفَر |

ảyna ảmteảatok? — أيْنَ أمْتِعَتُك؟

**where is your luggage?**

hal maảaka shay mamnuả. — هَلْ مَعكَ شَيْء مَمْنوع؟

**Do you have any forbidden thing?**

la yāsayyedi . — لا يا سَيِّدي.

**No, sir.**

beẻmkāneka ản tofattish. — بِإِمْكَانِكَ أنْ تُفَتّش .

**You can search.**

ẻftaḥ hādhehe lḥaqibata men faḍlek. — إفْتَح هَذِه الحَقِيبَةَ مِنْ فَضْلك .

**open this bag, please.**

be kol sorur, yā sāyyedi. — بِكُل سُرور يا سَيِّدي .

**With pleasure, sir.**

shokran maảa ssalamah. — شُكْراً مَع السَّلاّمة .

**Thank you, good-bye.**

# 38 At the Travel Agency

# في وكالة السَفَر 38

| | | |
|---|---|---|
| travel | ảssafar | السَّفَر |
| travel | yosāfer | يُسافر |
| by sea | baḥran | بَحْرًا |
| by land | barran | بَرًّا |
| by air | jawwan | جَوًّا |
| by train | belqeṭār | بالقِطار |

ỏfakker bessafar jawwan ẻla bāris. أُفَكِّر بالسَّفَر جَوًّا إلى باريس .

I am thinking of flying to Paris

mā heya lỏjur? ما هِيَ الأجُور؟ .

What are the fares? How much is the ticket?

maẩ ảyyat sharekah torid ản tosāfer? مَع أيَّةَ شَرِكَةْ تُرِيد أنْ تُسافِر؟

What company do you like to travel with?

hal el visa ṣāleḥah? هَل الڤيزا صالِحَة؟

Is your visa valid?

matā toqleẩo ṭṭāẻrah? مَتَى تُقْلِعُ الطَّائِرَة؟

When will the plane take off?

baaͨda sāaͨah. بَعْدَ ساعَةْ .

After an hour.

hal honak tawaqqof qabla bāris? هَل هُناكْ تَوَقُّف قَبْلَ بارِيس؟

Is there any stop before Paris?

naaͨam tawaqqof sāaͨatayn faqaṭ. نَعَمْ، تَوَقُّفْ ساعَتَيْن فَقَطْ .

Yes, two hours stop only .

yomkenoka lesterāḥah fe lotil. يُمْكِنُك الإسْتِراحَةْ في الأوُتيل .

You may have a rest in the hotel.

# 39 At The Hotel

# في الـفُـنْـدُق 39

| | | |
|---|---|---|
| In The Hotel | fel fondoq | في الفُنْدُق |
| hotel manager | modiro lfondoq | مُدير ُالفندُق |
| Where is the key of the room? | ảyna meftāho lgḥorfah? | أينَ مفْتاح الغُرْفة؟ |
| first class | darajah ỏulā | دَرَجَة أولى |
| sitting room | ghorfato lẻsterāḥah | غُرْفَة الإستِراحَة |
| bell-boy | khādem | خَادِم |
| blanket | ḥēram | حِرام |
| bed sheet | sharshaf | شَرْشَف |
| pillow | makhaddah | مَخَدَّة |
| bathroom | ḥammām | حَمَّام |

I want a single room. أريدُ غُرْفَةَ بسَرير واحد .

ỏrido ghorfah be sarir wāḥed.

I want a quiet room away of noise. أريدُها غُرْفَة هادئَة بَعيدَة عَن الضَّجَّة .

ỏridohā ghorfatan hādeảh baảidah ảneḍḍajjah.

Have you booked a room? هَل حَجزْتَ غُرْفَة؟

hal ḥajazta ghorfah?

How long would you like to stay? كَمْ تُريدْ أنْ تَبْقى ؟

kam torid ản tabqā?

I want to stay one week at least. أُريدُ أَنْ أَبْقى أُسْبوعًا على الأَقَلّ.

ὀrido ἀn ἀbqā ὀsbuᶜaan ᶜala lἀqall.

I will give you a room in the third floor. سَأعْطيك غُرْفَةً في الطَّابِقِ الثَّالِثْ.

saὀᶜṭika ghorfatan feṭṭābeqe ththāleth.

How much are the rates for one week? كَمْ الأجْرَةُ في الأَسْبُوعِ؟

kam elὀojrato fe lὀsbuᶜe?

$ 500 paid in advance. خَمْسُمائَةِ دولارْ، تُدْفَعُ مُقَدَّمًا.

khamsomeὀate dular todfaᶜo moqaddaman.

The porter will carry your cases immediately. أَلْحَمَّال سَيَنْقُلْ لَكَ حَقائِبَكَ حالاً.

ὀal ḥammāl sayanqol laka ḥaqāὀebaka ḥālan.

I would like to be woken at eight in the morning. أُفَضِّلُ أَنْ أوقَظَ في الثَّامِنَة صَبَاحًا

ὀofaḍḍelo ὀan ὀuqadha fe ththāmenate ṣabāḥan.

Would you like tea or coffee in the morning? أَتُحِبُّ الشَّاي أمِ القَهْوَةَ في الصَّباحْ؟

ὀatoḥebbo shshāya ame lqahw ata fe ṣṣabāḥ?

I would like coffee with cream. أُفَضِّلُ القَهْوَةَ معَ الحَليب.

ὀofaḍḍelo lqahwata maᶜa lḥalib.

Your order should arrive shortly after eight. سَيَصِلُ طَلَبُكَ بَعْدَ الثَّامِنَة بِقَليلْ.

sayaṣelo ṭalaboka baᶜda ththāmenate beqalil.

# 40 On The Bus — 40 في السَّيَّارة

On The Bus | fessayārah | في السَّيَّارة

Does this bus go to Beirut? | هَلْ هَذا الباصْ إلى بَيْروت؟

hal hādha lbāṣ ẻlā bayrut?

I want to get off near the museum. | أُريدُ أَنْ أَنْزِلَ قُرْبَ المَتْحَفْ .

ỏrido ản ảnzela qorba lmatḥaf.

I will put you off near it. | سَأُنْزِلُكَ قَريباً مِنْهُ .

sa ỏnzeloka qariban menho.

Thank you. | شُكراً لَكَ .

shokran laka.

How much is the fare to Beirut? | كَمِ الأجْرَةُ إلى بَيْروت؟

kame lỏjrato ẻlā bayrut?

Two thousand lebanese pounds only. | أَلْفا لَيْرَة لُبْنانيَّة فَقَطْ .

ảlfā lāyraten lobnāneyyaten faqaṭ.

When will we arrive to Beirut? | مَتَى نَصِلُ إلى بَيْرُوتْ؟

matā naṣelo ẻlā bayrut?

It will take one hour and a half. | سَتَأخُذ الطَّريقُ ساعَةْ ونِصفْ .

satảkhodho ṭṭariqo sāả̒ah wa neṣf.

Get off here, please. | إنْزِلْ هُنا مِنْ فَضْلَكْ .

ẻnzel honā men faḍlek.

Is the museum far away from here? | هَلِ المَتْحَف بَعيدْ مِنْ هُنا؟

hale lmatḥaf baả̒id men honā?

لا ، خَمْسونَ مِتْراً إلى الأمام، ثُمَّ بِضْعَة أمْتار إلى الشَّمال .

No, fifty meters forward, then turn to the left for a few meters.

la, khāmsuna metran ẻla lảmām, thomma beḍả̒at ảmtār ela shshāmal.

# 41 At The Post Office / في مَكْتَبِ البَريد

| | | |
|---|---|---|
| At The Post Office | fi maktabe lbarid | في مكْتَب البَريد |
| office | maktab | مكْتَب |
| post | barid | بَريد |
| letter | resālah | رِسَالَه |
| registered | maḍmunah | مَضْمونَه |
| urgent | mostaảjalah | مُسْتَعْجَله |
| telegram | barqeyyah | بَرْقِيَّة |
| post card | beṭāqah barideyyah | بِطاقَة بَريديَّة |
| post box | ṣonduq barid | صُنْدوق بَريد |
| envelope | ḍharf | ظَرْف |
| address | ảonwān | عُنْوان |
| sender | morsel | مُرْسِل |
| receiver | morsal ẻlayhe | مُرْسَل إلَيْه |
| postman | mowazzeảo lbarid | مُوَزّعُ البَريد |
| telephone | hātef | هاتِف |
| stamp | ṭābaảo barid | طابَعُ بَريد |
| parcel | ṭard | طَرْد |
| telephone call | mokhābarah | مُخابَرة |

I want to send a letter to... أُريدُ أنْ أرْسِلَ رِسَالةً إلى . . .

ỏrido ản ỏrsela resālatan ẻlā...

How much is the postage? كَمْ أجْرَةُ البَريد؟

kam ỏjrato lbarid?

It is three dollars. إنَّها ثَلاثَةُ دولاراتْ.

ẻnnahā thalāthato dulārāt.

How much is the postage of the registered letter? كَمْ أجْرَةُ الرِّسالَةِ المَضْمونَه؟

kam ỏjrato rresālate lmaḍmunah?

I want to send a telegram to... أُريدُ إرْسَال بَرْقيةٍ إلى . . .

ỏrido ẻrsāla barqeyyaten ẻlā...

What is the charge by the word? ما هِيَ أجْرَةُ الكَلِمَة؟

mā heya ỏjrato lkalimah?

I want to call... أُريد أنْ أتَّصِلَ تِلفونيًا بـ . . .

ỏrido ản ảttaṣela telefuneyyan be...

| | | |
|---|---|---|
| At The Restaurant | fil maṭåam | في المطعم |
| table | ṭāwelah | طاوِلَةْ |
| plate | ṣaḥn | صَحْن |
| fork | shawkah | شَوْكه |
| spoon | melåaqah | مِلْعَقه |
| knife | sekkin | سِكِّين |
| napkin | maḥramah | مَحْرَمه |
| breakfast | foṭur | فُطور |
| lunch | ghadā› | غَداء |
| dinner | åashā› | عَشاء |
| menu | lāeḥato ṭṭaåām | لائحَةُ الطَّعام |
| waiter | karsun | «كَرْسون» : نادِل |
| cheese | jebnah | جِبْنَه |
| egg | bayḍah | بَيْضَه |
| cakes | kaåk | كَعْك |
| peas | ḥommoṣ | حُمُّص |
| soup | shurba | شورْبا |
| chicken | dajāj | دَجاج |
| rice | rozz | رُزّ |
| beans | fāṣulia | فاصوليا |
| grilled meat | laḥm mashwi | لَحمْ مَشْوي |

| | | |
|---|---|---|
| fried chicken | farruj maqli | فَرُّوج مَقْلي |
| fish | samak | سَمَك |
| vegetables | khoḍār | خُضار |
| okra | bāmyah | بامْيَه |
| fruit | fākehah | فاكِهَه |
| beverages | moraṭṭebāt | مُرَطِّبات |
| bill | fāturah | فاتورَه |

o̓rid fenjān shāy maa̔ ḥalib, men faḍlek. أُريدْ فِنجْان شايْ مَعَ حَليبْ، مِن فَضْلَك .

I would like a cup of tea with milk, please.

o̓rid ṣaḥn dajāj maa̔ rozz. أُريدْ صَحْن دَجاج مَعْ رُزّ .

I would like a dish of chicken with rice.

o̓faḍḍel shurabata lkhoḍār أُفَضِّل شورَبَة الخُضار .

I prefer vegetable soup.

o̓faḍḍel koktila lfawākeh. أفَضِّل كوكتيلَ الفَواكِه .

I prefer fruit cocktail.

a̓khbere ṭṭāhi a̓n yosrea̔a, men faḍlek. أَخبِرِ الطَّاهي أن يُسْرِعَ مِنْ فَضْلِكْ .

Tell the chef to hurry, please.

a̓na jae̓a jeddan, wa shokran. أنَا جائع جِدًا، وَشُكراً .

I am starved. Thank you.

a̓a̔ṭeni fāturata lḥesāb, men faḍlek. أَعْطِني فاتورَةَ الحِساب، مِنْ فَضْلِك .

Give me the bill, please.

# 43 At The Bank

# فـي المَـصْـرَف 43

| | | |
|---|---|---|
| At The Bank | fil maṣref | في المَصْرِف |
| bank | maṣref | مَصْرِف |
| money order | ḥawālah | حَوالَه |
| cheque | shikk | شيك |
| money | māl-noqud | مال-نقُود |
| exchange rate | seảro ṣṣarf | سِعْرُ الصَّرْف |

mā howa seảro ṣarfe ddolare lảmriki? ما هو سِعرُ صَرْفِ الدُّولار الأمِيركي؟

What is the exchange rate of the American dollar?

ỏrido ản ảṣrefa hādha shshik. أُريدُ أنْ أصْرِفَ هَذا الشّيك .

I want to cash this cheque.

matā yaftaḥo lmaṣref? مَـتَـى يَفْـتَـحُ المَـصْـرِف؟

When does the bank open?

ảmino ṣṣonduq. أمِـينُ الـصُّـنْـدُوق .

cashier-teller.

ẻdfaả hādha shshikk. إدْفَعْ هَذا الشـيك .

Pay this cheque.

ٲrido ٲn ٲshtareya ٴaashrata ٲshom. أُريدُ أنْ أشْتَريَ عَشْرَةَ أسْهُم .

I want to buy ten shares.

ٲyna maktabo ṣṣayrafah? أيْنَ مكْتَبُ الصَّيْرَفه؟

Where is the exchange office?

ٳmḍe shshikka honā men faḍlek. إمْضِ الشيكَ هُنا مِن فَضْلك .

Sign the cheque here, please.

هَل مِنَ المُمْكِنْ أن تَصْرِفوا هَذِه الدُّولارات باللُّبْناني؟

hal mena lmomken ٲn taṣrefu hādhehe ddolarāt bel lobnāni?

Would you change these dollars for lebanese currency?

ٲrido ٲn ٲtaḥaqqa men seٴare ṣṣarf أُريدُ أنْ أتَحَقَّقَ مِنْ سِعْر الصَّرْف .

I will just check the rate of exchange.

High interest - fāٴedah mortafeٴaah. فائِدة مُرْتَفِعَه .

Low interest - fāٴedah monkhafeḍah. فائِدة مُنْخَفِضَه .

# 44 At The Pharmacy

# في الصَّيْدلِيَّة 44

| | | |
|---|---|---|
| At The Pharmacy | fi ṣṣaydaleyyah | في الصيدلية |
| medicine | dawāɂ | دَواء |
| cotton | qoṭon | قُطُن |
| dressing | ḍammādah | ضَمَّادَة |
| first-aid | ɂesɁāf ɂawwali | إسْعاف أوَّلي |
| suppository | taḥmilah | تَحْميلَه |
| cough | soɁāl | سُعال |
| tranquilizer | mosakken | مُسكّن |
| cold | rashḥ | رَشْح |
| aspirin packet | Ɂolbat ɂasperin | عُلْبَة أسْپْيرين |
| vitamin | vetamin | ڤيتامين |
| diarrhea | ɂeshāl | إسْهال |
| pain | ɂalam | ألَم |
| constipation | ɂemsāk | إمْساك |
| tooth paste | maɁjun ɂasnān | مَعْجون أسْنَان |
| tooth brush | forshāt ɂasnān | فُرْشاة أسْنَان |
| soft | nāɁem | ناعِم |
| hard | khashen | خَشِن |

| | | |
|---|---|---|
| scented soap | ṣābun moa̔aṭṭar | صابون مُعَطَّر |
| temperature | ḥarārah | حَرَارَه |

Give me an antiseptic, please. أعْطِني مَطَهِّرًا للجُرْح، مِنْ فَضْلِك.

ảa̔ṭeni moṭahheran liljorḥ, men faḍlek.

I feel I have a temperature. أشْعُرُ بِحَرَارَه.

ảsha̔oro beḥarārah.

I want a cough medicine. أريدُ دَواءً لِلسُّعال.

ỏrido dawāản lessoa̔āl.

Do you have a medicine for diarrhea? هَلْ عِنْدكَ دَواءٌ للإسْهال؟

hal a̔endaka dawāỏn leleshāl?

Do you have a medicine for constipation? هَلْ يوُجَدُ عِنْدكَ دَواءٌ للإمْساك؟

hal yujado a̔endaka dawāỏn leleṁsāk?

What doctor do you advise me to go to? إلى أيِّ طَبيبْ تَنْصَحُني بأنْ أذْهَب؟

ẻlā ảyye ṭabib tanṣaḥoni beản ảdhab?

# 45 At The Tobacconist — عند بائع الدخان 45

| | | |
|---|---|---|
| At The Tobacconist | ʿaenda bāʾeʿe ddokhkhān | عِنْدَ بائع الدُّخَّان . |
| good morning | ṣabāḥo lkhayr | صَباحُ الخَيْر |
| good evening | masāʾo lkhayr | مَسَاءُ الخَيْر |
| good afternoon | | |

Do you have cigarettes of this kind? هَلْ عِنْدَكَ سَجَائِرٌ مِنْ هَذا النَّوْع؟

hal ʿaendaka sajāʾer men hādha nnawʿa?

How much is the pack? ما سِعْرُ العُلْبَة؟

mā seʿaro laʿolbah?

How much is the box? ما ثمن الكروز؟

mā thamano lkruz?

It is very expensive. إنَّه غالٍ جِداً .

ʾennaho ghālen jeddan.

Give me one pack only, please. أعْطِني عُلْبَةً واحِدةً فَقَطْ ، منْ فَضْلِك .

ʾaʿaṭeni ʿaolbatan wāḥedatan faqaṭ, men faḍlek.

Thank you. ʾashkorok أشْكُرك .

# 46 At The Barber's Shop　　　عِـنْـدَ الحَـــــلاَّق 46

At The Barber's Shop　　　åendal ḥāllaq　　　عِنْدَ الحلاَّق

Good morning　　　ṣabāḥo lkhayr　　　صَباحُ الخَيْر

I want to have my hair cut.　　　أريدُ ؟أنْ أقُصَّ شَعْـري .

ỏrido ản ảqoṣṣa shaåri.

I want to shave, too.　　　أريدُ أنْ أحْلِقَ أيْضاً .

ỏrido ản ảḥleqa ảyḍan.

Take a seat, please.　　　إجْلِسْ مِن فَضْلَك .

ẻjles men faḍlek.

Lean back a little.　　　إسْنِدْ إلى الخَلْفِ قَليلاً .

ẻsned ẻla lkhalfe qalilan.

Your hair is long.　　　shaåroka ṭawil.　　　شَعْرُكَ طَويل .

Do you want me to cut it short for you?　　　أتُريدُني أن أقُصِّرَه لَكَ؟

åtoridoni ản ỏqaṣṣeraho laka?

Yes, a little bit.　　　naåam, qaṣṣerho qalilan　　　نَعَمْ، قَصِّرهُ قَليلاً

I want to <u>trim</u> my moustache.　　　أريد أن أشَذِّبَ شارِبي .

ỏrido ản ỏshadhdheba shārebi.

I want shampoo after the hair cut, please. أريدُ شامبو بَعْدَ القَصّ، مِنْ فَضْلِك .

ổrido shampu baẩda lqaṣṣ, men faḍleq.

I have a good <u>tonic</u> for dry hair. عِنْدِي مُقَوِّي جَيِّد للشَّعْر الجافّ .

ẩendi moqawwi jayyed leshshaẩre ljäff.

Well, I'll try it ḥasanan, saổjarreboho حَسَنًا سأجَرِّبهُ .

How much do you want, please? kam torid men faḍlek كَم تُريد مِنْ فَضْلِك؟

Thank you. shokran laka. شُكْرًا لَكَ .

# 47 Making An Appointment

# تَحْديد مَوْعِد 47

| | | |
|---|---|---|
| Making An Appointment | taḥdido mawa̔ed | تحديد موعد |
| Good morning | ṣabāḥo lkhayr | صَباحُ الخَيْر |

Is this Mr .... office ? هَلْ هَذا مكْتَبُ السَّيِّد. . . ؟

hal hādhā maktabo ssayyed ....?

I am .... I want to see .... today. أنا . . . . أريدُ مُقابَلةْ . . . . اليوم

a̓nā ... o̓rido moqābalat .... a̓lyawm.

Sorry. Mr... is very busy to-day. آسِفه. السَّيِّد . . . . مَشْغول جِدًا اليَوْم.

a̓ sefah. a̓ssayyed .... mashghul jeddane lyawm

You have to make a new appointment. عَلَيْكَ أنْ تَحْصَل على مَوْعِدْ جَديد .

a̔alayka a̓n taḥṣala a̔alā mawa̔ed jadid.

O.K. make me another appiontment. حَسَنًا حَدِّدي لي مَوْعِدًا آخَرْ .

ḥasanan. ḥaddedi li mawa̔edan a̓ākhar.

Is Friday... o'clock suitable? هَلْ يَوْمُ الجُمْعَة السَّاعَة. . . مُناسِب؟

hal yawm ljoma̔ah a̓ssā̔aah... monāseb?

Yes, that would be quite all right. نَعَم ، ذلِكَ مُناسب تَمامًا .

na̔am dhāleka monāseb tamāman.

Thank you very much, madam. أشْكُرُكِ كَثيراً ، سَيِّدَتي .

a̔shkoroke kathiran, sayyedati.

# 48 Food — الطّعام

| | | |
|---|---|---|
| Food | ȧṭṭaåām | ألطّعام |
| eggs | bayḍ | بَيْض |
| boiled eggs | bayḍ masluq | بَيْض مَسْلوق |
| fried eggs | bayḍ maqli | بَيْض مَقْلي |
| scrambled eggs | bayḍ makhfuq | بَيْض مَخفوق |
| cheese | jebnah | جِبْنَةْ |
| nuts | jaws | جَوْز |
| milk | ḥalib | حَليب |
| sweets | ḥalwayāt | حَلْويات |
| olive oil | zayt zaytun | زَيت زَيْتون |
| corn oil | zayt dhorah | زَيْت ذُرَه |
| olives | zaytun | زَيْتون |
| sugar | sokkar | سُكَّر |
| fish | samak | سَمَك |
| fat | samnah | سَمْنَه |
| tea | shāy | شاي |
| honey | åasal | عَسَل |
| chicken | farruj | فَرّوج |

| | | |
|---|---|---|
| meat | laḥm | لَحْم |
| beef | laḥm åejl | لَحْم عِجْل |
| yog(h)urt | labnah (laban moṣaffā) | لبنَة (لَبَن مُصَفّى) |
| jam | morabbā | مُرَبّى |
| salt | melḥ | مِلْح |
| butter | zebdah | زِبْدَة |
| cream | qashṭah | قَشْطَه |
| breakfast | foṭur | فُطور |
| lunch | ghadāɔ | غَداء |
| dinner | åashāɔ | عَشاء |
| omelet | åejjah | عِجَّه |
| sausage | maqāneq | مَقانِق |
| hungry | jāɔeå | جائِع |

# 49 Fruits and Vegetables

# الفواكه والخضار 49

| | | |
|---|---|---|
| Fruits and Vegetables | ảlfawākeh walkhoḍār | ألفوَاكِه والخُضَار |
| pear | ẻjāṣ | إجَاص |
| orange | bortoqāl | بُرْتُقال |
| onion | baṣal | بَصَل |
| melon | baṭṭikh | بَطّيخ |
| parsley | baqdunes | بَقْدونِس |
| dates | balaḥ | بَلَح |
| tomatoes | banadurah | بَنَدورَة |
| apples | toffāḥ | تُفّاح |
| dried dates | tamr | تَمْر |
| figs | tin | تين |
| garlic | thum | ثُوم |
| carrots | jazar | جَزَر |
| lemon - lime | ḥāmeḍ | حامِض |
| lettuce | khass | خَسّ |
| plum | khukh | خوخ |
| cucumber | kheyār | خيار |
| peach | dorrāq | دُرّاق |
| pomegranate | rommān | رُمّان |
| quince | safarjal | سَفَرْجَل |
| salad | salaṭah | سَلَطة |

| | | |
|---|---|---|
| spinach | sabānekh | سَبانِخ |
| beet | shamandar | شَمَنْدَر |
| thyme | ṣaȃtar | صَعْتَر |
| grapes | ȃenab | عِنَب |
| strawberry | friz | فْريز |
| radish | fejel | فِجِل |
| cauliflower | qarnabiṭ | قَرْنَبيط |
| cherries | karaz | كَرَز |
| celery | krafs | كْرَفس |
| almond | lawz | لَوْز |
| apricot | moshmosh | مُشْمُش |
| cabbage | malfuf | مَلفُوف |
| banana | mawz | مَوْز |
| mint | naȃnāȃ | نَعْناع |
| tangerine | yusof ȃfandi | يوسُف أفَنْدي |
| okra | bāmeyah | بامِيَه |
| potato | baṭāṭā | بطَاطا |
| eggplant | bādhenjān | باذِنْجان |
| mallow | khobbayzah | خُبَّيزَة |
| pumpkin | qarȃ | قَرْع |
| coriander | kozbarah | كُزْبَرَة |
| squash | kusā | كوسَى |
| turnip | left | لِفْت |
| pepper | felfel | فِلْفِل |

| | | |
|---|---|---|
| Seeds - grains | bodhur - ḥobub | ألْبُذور - ألْحبُوب |
| rice | ảrozz | أرُزّ |
| pea-pease | bāzella | بازيلاّ |
| bruised wheat | borghol | بُرْغُل |
| chick-pease | ḥommoṣ | حُمُّص |
| maze | dhorah | ذُرَه |
| lentil | ảadas | عَدَس |
| beans | ful | فول |
| pea-nut | ful sudāni | فول سوداني |
| pistachio | fostoq | فُسْتُق |
| beans | fāṣulya | فاصولْيا |
| wheat | qamḥ | قَمْح |
| lupine | tormos | تُرْمُس |
| barley | shaảir | شَعير |
| oats | shufān | شوفان |

# Beverages, drinks

# ألْمَشْروبات



| | | |
|---|---|---|
| Beverages, drinks | ảlmashrubāt | ألْمَشْروبات |
| water | māʾ | ماء |
| milk | ḥalib | حَليب |
| tea | shāy | شاي |
| juice | ʿaaṣir | عَصير |
| coffee | qahwah | قَهْوَةْ |
| cacao | kākāw | كاكاو |
| lemonade | lemonāḍah | لموناضَه |
| fruit cocktail | ʿaaṣiro lfawākeh | عَصير ألْفَوَاكِه |
| soft drinks | moraṭṭebāt | مُرَطِّبات |
| anise | yansun | يانْسون |

I am very thirsty. – أنا عَطْشانْ جِداً .

ảna ʿaaṭshān jeddan

I want to drink... . – أريدُ أنْ أشْرَب . . . .

ỏrido ản ʾashrab... .

| | | |
|---|---|---|
| Animals | ͗alḥayawānāt | ألْحَيَوانات |
| lion | ͗asad | أسَد |
| rabbit | ͗arnab | أرْنَب |
| snake | ͗afʿaā | أفْعَى |
| cow | baqarah | بَقَرة |
| mule | baghl | بَغْل |
| owl | bum | بوم |
| crocodile | temsāḥ | تِمسْاح |
| bull,ox | thawr | ثَورْ |
| fox | thaʿalab | ثَعْلَب |
| camel | jamal | جَمَل |
| buffalo | jāmus | جاموس |
| horse | ḥeṣan | حِصان |
| donkey | ḥemar | حِمار |
| lamb | ḥamal | حَمَل |
| pig | khanzir | خَنْزير |
| bear | dobb | دُبّ |

| | | |
|---|---|---|
| wolf | dheʾb | ذئْب |
| fish | samak | سَمَك |
| turtle | solaḥafāt | سُلَحْفاة |
| hyena | ḍaboʿa | ضَبُع |
| goat | ʿaanzah | عَنْزَةْ |
| gazelle, deer | ghazāl | غَزال |
| mare | faras | فَرَس |
| leopard | fahd | فَهْد |
| elephant | fil | فيل |
| monkey | qerd | قِرْد |
| dog | kalb | كَلْب |
| ram | kabsh | كَبْش |
| bitch | kalbah | كَلْبَةْ |
| hound | kalb saluqi | كَلْبَ سَلوقي |
| tiger | namer | نَمر |
| ewe | naʿajah | نَعْجَةْ |
| cat | herr-qeṭṭ | هِرّ-قِطّ |
| rhinoceros | waḥid lqarn | وَحيد القَرْن |

## 53 Birds — ألطُّيور

| Birds | aṭṭoyur | ألطُّيور |
|---|---|---|
| parrot | babbaghā | بَبّغاء |
| nightingale | bolbol | بُلْبُل |
| duck | baṭṭah | بَطّه |
| partridge | ḥajal | حَجَل |
| goldfinch | ḥassun | حَسّون |
| pigeon | ḥamāmah | حَمامَه |
| cock | dik | ديك |
| hen | dajājah | دَجاجَةْ |
| swallow | senunu | سِنونو |
| blackbird | shaḥrur | شَحْرور |
| peacock | ṭāwus | طاووس |
| crow | ghorāb | غُراب |
| butterfly | farāshah | فَراشة |
| lark | qobbarah | قُبَّرة |

---

| turkey | dik ḥabash | ديك حَبَش |
|---|---|---|
| falcon | ṣaqr | صَقْر |

| | | |
|---|---|---|
| crane | karki | كَرْكي |
| stork | laqlaq | لَقْلَق |
| heron | mālek ảlḥazin | مالِك أَلحزَين |
| eagle | nasr | نَسْر |
| ostrich | naảāmah | نَعامَةْ |
| hoopoe | hodhod | هُدْهُد |
| bat | waṭwāṭ | وَطْواط |
| goose | wazzah | وَزَّةْ |

---

| | | |
|---|---|---|
| tame | ảlif-dājen | أَليف داجِن |
| wild | barri | بَرِّي |
| warbling | taghrid | تَغْريد |
| feather | rishah | ريشَةَ |
| nest | ảoshsh | عُشّ |
| bill | menqār | مِنْقار |
| wing | janāḥ | جَناح |

| | | |
|---|---|---|
| Fish | ả lả smāk | الأسْماك |
| octobus | ảkhṭabuṭ | أخْطَبوط |
| whiting | buri | بوري |
| crocodile | temsāḥ | تمسْاح |
| tuna (tunny) | tonn | تُنّ |
| whale | ḥut | حوت |
| eel | ḥanklis | حَنْكليس |
| dolphin | dolphin | دُلْفين |
| salmon | samak solaymān | سَمَك سُلَيْمان |
| sardine | sardin | سَرْدين |
| crab | salṭaảun-saraṭān | سَلْطَعون / سَرَطان |
| sole | samak musā | سَمَك موسىَ |
| tortoise | solaḥfāh | سُلَحْفاه |
| red mullet | solṭān ẻbrāhim | سُلْطان إبْراهيم |
| shark | qersh | قِرْش |
| shrimp | qraydes | قُرَيْدس |
| lobster | karakand | كَرْكَنْد |
| fins | zaảānef | زَعانف |
| scales | ḥarāshef | حَراشِف |
| gills | khayāshim | خَياشيم |

| | | |
|---|---|---|
| In The Market | fissuq | في السُّوق |
| trousers | banṭalun | بَنْطَلون |
| blouse | bluzah | بْلوزَه |
| bag | jazdān | جَزْدان |
| shoes | ḥedhāᵓ | حذاء |
| slipper | shebsheb | شِبْشِب |
| bodice | ṣedreyyah | صِدْرِيَّةْ |
| suit | ṭaqm | طَقْم |
| shirt | qamiṣ | قَميص |
| coat | meᶜṭaf | مِعْطَف |
| stockings | kalsāt | كَلسْات |
| I want this suit. | ᵓorido hadha ṭṭaqm. | أريدُ هَذا الطَّقْم. |
| I want to try it. | ᵓorido ᵓan ᵓojarrebaho. | أريدُ أنْ أجَـرِّبَهُ. |

tight : ضَيِّق، wide, loose : واسِع، try : يُجَرِّب، fitting room: غُرْفَةُ القياس

suitable: مُناسِب

Where is the fitting room? أَينَ غُرْفَةُ القِياس؟

ảyna ghorfato lqeyās?

This suit is tight. هَذا الطَّقْمُ ضَـيِّق .

hādha ṯtaqmo ḍayyeq.

I want a wider suit. أريدُ طَقـمًا أوْسَعْ .

ỏrido ṭaqman ảwsaả.

This is suitable. هَذا مُناسِب .

hādhā monāseb

How much is it? kam seảroho كَمْ سِعْرُهُ؟
What is its price?

It is expensive. ẻnnaho ghālen إنَّهُ غالٍ .

I want a cheaper one. ỏrido nawảan ảrkhaṣ أرِيدُ نَـوْعًا أرْخَص .

This is the bill. hādhehe heya fāturato lḥesāb هَذه هِيَ فاتورَةُ الحِساب .

ألسِّعْرُ مائَةْ وَخَمْسونْ دولار . حَسْمُ عَشْرُ دولارات .

The price is one hundred and fifty dollars. Ten dollars discount.

ảsseảr meảh wakhamsun dullār. Ḥasm ảashrat dularāt.

Thank you. Shokran شُكْـراً .

You're welcome. ảhlan wasahlan أهْلاً وَسَهْلاً .

---

Want: أُريد - price: سِعْر – ثَمَن - expensive: غالٍ - cheaper: أرْخَص

cheap: رَخيص - rakhiṣ - discount: حَسْم - welcome: أهْلاً وَسَهْلاً

# 56 With the jeweller

# عِنْدَ الصَّائِغ
# الجَوْهَرْجِي

**ȁenda ṣṣaȇgh - ȁl jawharji**

| | | |
|---|---|---|
| diamond | ȁlmās | أَلماس |
| platinum | blātin | بْلاتين |
| gold | dhahab | ذَهَب |
| agate | ȁaqiq | عَقيق |
| cornelian | ȁqiq aḥmar | عَقيق أَحْمَر |
| turquoise | fayruz | فَيْروز |
| silver | feḍḍah | فِضَّه |
| pearl | lȍlȍ | لُؤْلِؤ |
| ruby | yāqut | ياقوت |
| ring | khātam | خاتَم |
| bracelet | ȇswārah | إسْوارَه |
| ear - rings | ḥalaq | حَلَق |
| neck-lace | ȁoqd | عُقْد |

Where is the jewellery market please? أَيْنَ يوجَدُ سوقُ الصَّاغَه، مِنْ فَضْلِك؟

ȁyna yujado suqo ṣṣāghah men faḍlek?

Is it far from here? هَلْ هُوَ بَعيد مِنْ هُنا؟

hal howa baȁid men honā?

---

jeweller: صائِغ ، جَوْهَرْجي - market : سُوق - far: بَعيد - here: هُنا

accompany: يُرافِق

Can you accompany me? هَلْ تَسْتَطيعُ أنْ تُرافِقَني؟

hal tastaṭiʿao ʾan torāfeqani?

With pleasure, sir. بِكُلِّ سُرورْ، سَيِّدي.

bekoll sorur, sayyedi.

Can I try this ring? هَلْ أسْتَطيعُ أنْ أجَرِّبَ هَذا الخاتَم؟

hal ʾastaṭiʿao ʾan ʾojarreba hādha lkhātam?

Of course. ṭabʿan طَبْعًا.

I am thinking of presenting it to my friend. أفكِّرُ بِأنْ أهْديه لِصَديقي.

ʾofakkero beʾan ʾahdihe le ṣadiqi

How much shall I pay? Kʿam ʾalayya ʾan ʾadfaʿa? كَمْ عَلَيَّ أنْ أدْفَعَ؟

It is a bit expensive. ʾennaho ghālen qalilan. إنَّهُ غالٍ، قَليلاً.

Show me that neck-lace. ʾareni dhāleka lʿoqd. أرِني ذَلِكَ العُقْد.

It is beautiful, how much is it? إنَّهُ جَميلْ، كَمْ ثَمَنُه؟

ʾennaho jamil, kam thamanoh?

Well, I shall buy it. ḥasanan saʾashtarih. حَسَنًا، سَأشْتَريه.

Wrap it for me, please. loffaho li men faḍlek. لُفَّهُ لي مِنْ فَضْلِك.

Thank you, very much. shokran, kathiran jeddan. شُكْرًا، كَثيرًا جِدًا.

---

pleasure: سرور - sir: سيّد - can: أستطيع ، أقدر - present: أهدي - pay: أدفع

a bit: قليلاً - well: حسنًا - wrap: يلفّ - very much: كثيرًا جدًا - think: أفكّر

# 57 With the tailor — عِنْدَ الخَيّاط 57

ʿaenda lkhayyāṭ

| | | |
|---|---|---|
| sew | yakhiṭ | يَخيط |
| suit | ṭaqm | طَقْم |
| cloth | qemāsh | قِماش |
| fitting | bruvah | بْروڤَه |
| button | zerr | زرّ |

أريدُكَ أنْ تخيطَ لي طَقْماً مِنْ هذا القِماش .

I want you to sew a suit for me from this cloth.

ʾoridoka ʾan takhiṭa li ṭaqman men hādha lqemāsh.

When is the fitting? matā satakuno lbruvah? متى ستكونُ البروڤَه؟

After ten days. baʿada ʿaashrat ʾayyām. بَعْدَ عَشْرَةْ أيّام .

This jacket is long. hādhehe ljāket ṭawilah. هَذِهِ الجاكيت طَويلَةْ .

Can you shorten it a little for me? هَلْ تَسْتَطيعُ أنْ تُقَصِّرَها لي قَليلاً؟

hal tastaṭiʿao ʾan toqaṣṣerahā li qualilan?

---

day: يَوْم - days: أيّام - long:طَويلَةْ - sleeves:أكْمام - short:قَصيرَةْ - shorten:يُقَصِّر
lengthen:يُطَوِّل - trousers:بَنْطَلون - loosen: وَسِّع

الأكْمامْ قَصِيرةْ، طَوّلْها قَليلاً مِنْ فَضْلك .

The sleeves are short, lengthen them a little, please.

ảl ảkmām qaṣirah, ṭawwilhā qalilan men faḍlek.

The trousers are tight, loosen them a litle. البَنْطلونُ ضَيِّق، وَسِّعْهُ قَليلاً .

ảlbanṭaluno ḍayyeq, wasseảho qalilan.

Try it another time. جَرّبْهُ مَرَّةً أُخْرى .

jarrebho marratan ảkhrā.

Do you want me to pay now? أتريدُني أنْ أدْفَع الآن؟

ảtoridoni ản ảdfaảa lản?

Do you accept personal cheque? هَلْ تَقْبَلُ شيكًا شَخْصِيًّا؟

hal taqbalo shikan shakhṣeyyan?

Pay half the costs now. إدْفَعْ نِصفَ التَّكاليفَ الآن .

ẻdfaả neṣfa ttākālif lản

وَالنِّصفُ الآخَرِ عِنْدَما تَسْتَلِمُ الطَّقْم .

And the other half when you receive the suit .

wannesfo lảkhar ảendamā tastalemo ṭṭaqm.

---

pay: أدْفَع - another: أخْرى، آخر - accept: تَقْبَل - personal: شَخْصِيّ - cheque: شيك

half: نِصْف - costs: تكَاليف

# 58 With the Grocer

ẩenda ssamān - lbaqqāl

# 58 عِنْدَ السَّمان البَقّال

| | | |
|---|---|---|
| grocer | sammān -baqqāl | سَمّان – بَقّال |
| butter | zobdah | زُبْدَه |
| cheese | jebnah | جِبْنَه |
| bread | khobz | خُبْز |
| rice | rozz | رُزّ |
| olives | zaytun | زَيْتون |
| fat | samnah | سَمْنَه |
| sugar | sokkar | سُكَّر |
| tea | shāy | شاي |
| soap | ṣābun | صَابون |
| honey | ẩasal | عَسَل |
| juice | ẩaṣir | عَصير |
| pepper | felfel | فِلْفِل |
| coffee | qahwah | قَهْوَة |
| almonds | lawz | لَوْز |
| napkins | maḥārem waraq | مَحارِم وَرَق |

Do you have cheese? هَل عِنْدك جِبْنه؟

hal a̔endaka jebnah?

Give me half a kilo of cheese. أَعْطِني نِصْف كيلو جِبْنَه .

a̓a̔ṭeni neṣf kilu jebnah

Do you have good quality honey? هَلْ عِنْدك عَسَلٌ جَيِّد؟

hal a̔endaka a̔asalon jayyed?

How much is a kilo? كَمْ ثَمَنُ الكيلو؟

kam thamano lkilu?

Give me a tin of sardin. أَعْطِني عُلْبَة سَرْدين .

a̓a̔ṭeni a̔olbata sardin

هَلْ أَسْتَطيعُ أَنْ أرى تاريخَ الصُّنْعِ وتاريخَ الانْتِهاءِ؟

can I see the manufacturing and the expiry date?

hal a̓staṭia̔o a̓n a̓rā tārikha ṣṣona̔e wal e̓ntehāɔ ?

I want a packet of napkins. أُريدُ عُلْبَة مَحارِم .

o̓rido a̔olbata maḥarem .

I want a tin of milk of a good quality. أُريدُ عُلْبَة حَليبْ مِنَ الجِنْسِ الجَيِّد .

o̓rido a̔olbata ḥalib mena ljense ljayyed

---

tin: عُلْبَةْ - manufacturing date: تاريخ الصُّنْع - expiry date:تاريخ الإنْتِهاء

good: جَيِّد - quality : (صِنْف ، جِنْس)

# With the clothes Salesman

# عِنْدَ بائِعِ المَلابِس

ʿaenda bāʾeʿae lmalābes



| | | |
|---|---|---|
| blouse | bluzah | بْلوزَه |
| hat | bornayṭah | بُرْنَيْطَه |
| men's hat | bornayṭah rejjāleyyah | برنيطة رجّاليَّه |
| women's hat | bornayṭah nesāʾeyyah | برنيطة نسائِيَّةْ |
| skirt | tannurah | تَنوّرَةْ |
| jacket-coat | meʿaṭaf | مِعْطَفْ |
| socks | jawāreb | جَوارِب |
| silk | ḥarir | حَرير |
| threads-strings | khitān | خيطان |
| button | zerr | زِرّ |
| belt | zennār | زِنّار |
| wool | ṣuf | صُوف |
| dress | fostān | فُسْتان |
| hat | qobbaʿaah | قُبَّعَهْ |
| shirt | qamiṣ | قَميص |
| gloves | qoffāz | قُفّاز |

tie: كْراڤَة ، رَبْطة = rabṭah - girdle: مَشَدّ mashad - cloth: قِماش qemash

swimming - suit: «مايوه» mayuh

| | | |
|---|---|---|
| over coat | kabbut | كَبّوت |
| linen | kettān | كِتّان |
| stockings | kalsāt | كَلسْات |
| sweater | kanzah | كَنْزَه |
| handkerchief | mendil | مِنْديل |
| towel | menshafah | مِنْشَفَه |
| napkin | fuṭah-mendil māẻdah | فوطَه – منْديل مائدَةْ |

How much is the meter of this cloth? ما ثَمنُ المِتْر مِنْ هذا القِماش؟

mā thamano lmetr men hātha lqemāsh?

It is expensive. I want a cheaper one. إنَّه غال. أريدُ نَوْعًا أرْخَص.

ẻnnaho ghālen, ỏrido nawẳan ẳrkhaṣ

What is the final price of this thing? ما هُوَ السِّعْرُ الأخيرُ لهذا الغَرَض؟

mā howa sseẳro lẳkhir lehādha lgharaḍ?

Show me the neck ties. أرني كْرافات – رَبْطاتِ العُنُق.

ẳreni krafāt - rabṭate lẳonoq.

I want three silk ties. أريدُ ثَلاثَ كَراڤاتْ حَرير.

ỏrido thalātha krafāt ḥarir.

I want woollen stockings, too. أريدُ جَوارِبَ صوفْ أيْضًا.

ỏrido jawareba ṣuf ẳyḍan.

How much are these cotton socks? كَمْ ثَمَنُ هذهِ الجوارِب القُطْنِيَّه؟

Kam thamano hādhehe ljawārebe lqoṭneyyah?

---

thing: غَرَض – شَيْء - final:الأخِير - too:أيْضًا - cotton:قُطْن ، قُطْني

# 60 At the clinic

fe laۜeyādah

# في العيادة 60

| | | |
|---|---|---|
| doctor | ṭabib | طَبيب |
| secretary | sekretirah | سكْرتيره |
| nurse | momarreḍah | مُمَرّضَة |
| urine | bawl | بوْل |
| blood | damm | دَمّ |
| medicine | dawāͻ | دَواء |
| analysis | taḥlil | تَحْليل |
| examination | faḥṣ | فَحْص |
| x-ray photograph | ṣurat ȃsheۜȃah | صُورَةْ أشعِّةْ |
| lung | reȃh | رئَة |
| kidney | kelyah | كلْيَةْ |
| back | ḍhahr | ظَهْر |
| pain | ȃlam | ألَم |

I feel pain in my back. أشْعُر بألَمُ في ظَهْري .

ȃshۜaor beȃlam fi ḍhahri

---

cold: رَشْح - bad: قَويّ ، سَيِئّ - pain: ألَم - feel: أشْعُر - temperature: حَرارَة

pulsation: نَبْض ، دقّات القلَب - allergy: حَساسِيه

I'll take your temperature. سَآخُذُ حرارَتك.

saa̓khodho ḥarāratak

I'll examine your pulsation. سَأفْحص نُبْضَكْ - دقّات قَلْبك.

saa̓fḥaṣo nabḍak - daqqāt qalbek

I have had a bad cold. أصِبْتُ بِرَشْحٍ قَوِيّ.

o̓ṣebto berashḥen qawii.

I have allergy to aspirine. عنْدي حَساسِيَّةْ للأسْبرين.

a̔endi ḥasaseyyah lela̓sperin.

I'll write you a prescription. سَأكْتُبُ لَكَ وَصْفَةْ طِبِّيَّةْ.

saa̓ktobo laka waṣfah ṭebbeyyah

Use the medicine for a week. إسْتَعْمِلِ الدَّواء لِـمُدَّة أسْبوع.

e̓staa̔mele ddawāɔ lemoddat o̓sbua̔.

You have to rest for five days. عَلَيْكَ أنْ تَرتاحَ لِمُدَّة خَمْسَةْ أيّام.

a̔alayka a̓n tartāḥa lemoddat khamsat a̓yyām

Let me see you after a week. دَعْني أراكَ بَعْدَ أسْبوع.

daa̔ni a̓rāka baa̔da o̓sbua̔.

---

rest: تَرْتاح - let me: دَعْني - see: أرَى - see you: أراك

# illness and Diseases

## ȧlmaraḍ walȧmrāḍ

# المَرَض والأمْـــراض



| | | |
|---|---|---|
| pain | ȧlam - wajaả | أَلَمْ - وَجَعْ |
| diarrhea | ẻshāl | إسْهال |
| croup | ȧbu kaảb | ابو كَعْب |
| constipation | ẻmsāk | إمْساك |
| dumb | ȧkhras | أخْرَس |
| deaf | ȧṭrash | أطْرَش |
| lame | ȧảraj | أعْرَج |
| blind | ȧảmā | أعْمَى |
| hoarseness | baḥḥah | بَحَّهْ |
| leprosy | baraṣ | بَرَص |
| henbane | benj | بِنْج |
| urine | bawl | بَوْل |
| typhoid | tefuẻid | تيفوئيد |
| vaccination | talqiḥ | تَلْقيح |
| small-pox | jadari | جَدَري |
| wound | jorḥ | جُرْح |
| measles | ḥaṣbah | حَصْبَه |
| diet | ḥemyah | حِمْيَةْ |
| fever | ḥommā | حُمَّى |
| dizziness | dawkhah | دَوْخَه |
| abscess | dommal | دُمَّل |

| | | |
|---|---|---|
| medicine | dawāɔ | دَواء |
| bruise | raḍḍah | رَضَّه |
| appendix | zāɔ̈edah | زائِدَه |
| cancer | saraṭan | سَرَطان |
| cough | saʿ̊alah | سَعْلَه |
| diabetes | sokkari | سُكَّري |
| bandage | ḍammād | ضَمَّاد |
| health | ṣeḥḥah | صِحَّةْ |
| plague | ṭāʿ̊un | طاعون |
| vaccine | ṭoʿ̊am | طُعْم |
| treatment | ʿ̊elāj | عِلاج |
| operation | ʿ̊amaleyyah | عَمَلِيَّةْ |
| sweat | ʿ̊araq | عَرَقْ |
| excrement | ghāɔ̈eṭ | غائِط |
| paralysis | fālej | فالِج |
| hernia | fetāq | فِتاق |
| vomitting | qayɔ | قَيْء |
| fractures | kosur | كُسور |
| patient | mariḍ | مَريض |

---

headache: صُداع ṣodāʿ̊ - rheumatism: وَجَعْ مَفاصِل wajaʿ̊ mafāṣel

toothache: وَجَعْ أَسْنان wajaʿ̊ ɔ̈asnān - scrab: جَرَب jarab

| | | |
|---|---|---|
| thermometer | mizān ḥarārah | ميزان حَرَاره |
| purgative | moshel | مُسْهِل |
| colic | maghṣ | مَغْص |
| recovery | naqāhah | نَقَاهه |

You must go to the hospital. عَلَيْكَ أنْ تَدْخُلَ المستَشْفى .

ἀalayka ȧn tadkhola lmostashfā.

How many days shall I stay there? كَمْ يوْمًا سَأبْقى هنُاك؟

Kam yawman saȧbqā honāk?

For some days only. لِبِضْعَةِ أيَّامٍ فَقَطْ .

lebeḍἀate ȧyyāmen faqaṭ.

You have to go on a diet. عَلَيْكَ أنْ تَتبَّعَ الحِمْيَةْ .

ἀalayka ȧn tattabeἀa lḥemyah.

I'll give you a list of the forbidden things. سَأعطِيكَ قائِمَةْ بالأشْياءِ المَمْنوعَةْ .

saȯἀṭika qāemah belȧshyāe lmamnuἀah .

---

stay: أَبْقَي - there: هُناك - some: بَضْعَةْ (بعضْ) - only: فَقَط - go on: يَتبَّعِ

diet: حَمْيَةْ - list: قائمَةْ - forbidden: مَمْنوعَةْ (ممْنوع)

# 62 At Home في البيت 62

| | | |
|---|---|---|
| at home | fe lbayt | في البَيْت |
| furniture | ảthāth | أثاث |
| floor | ảrḍo lghorfah | أرْضُ الغُرْفَه |
| door | bāb | باب |
| gate | bawwābah | بَوَّابَه |
| sewer | bāluảah | بالوعَه |
| wall | ḥāẻṭ | حائِط |
| bath-room | ḥammam | حَمَّام |
| mat | ḥaṣirah | حَصيره |
| blanket | ḥerām | حِرام |
| cupboard | Khezānah | خِزانَه |
| stairs | daraj | دَرَج |
| corner | zāweyah | زاوِيَةْ |
| curtains | satāẻr | سَتَائِر |
| cradle | sarir | سَرير |

---

pool: بركَةْ - veranda شُرْفَةْ - tap: حَنَفيّه

shelf: رَفّ - corridor: مَمَرّ بين الغُرَف (كوردور)

| | | |
|---|---|---|
| roof | saqf | سَقْف |
| ceiling | saṭḥ | سَطْح |
| ladder | sollam | سُلَّم |
| carpet | sejjādah | سِجَّادَه |
| sheet | sharshaf | شَرْشَف |
| window | shobbak | شُبَّاك |
| drawing-room | ṣālah | صالَةْ |
| storey | ṭābeq | طابق |
| threshold | ʿaatabah | عَتَبَةْ |
| column | ʿaamud | عَمود |
| lock | ghāl(qefl) | غال (قِفْل) |
| oven | forn | فُرْن |
| tiles | qermid | قِرْميد |
| bar | qaḍib ḥadid | قَضيب حَديد |
| counter pane (quilt) | leḥāf | لِحاف |
| entrance | madkhal | مَدْخَل |
| seat | maqʿaad | مَقْعَد |
| passage | mamarr | مَمَرّ |
| pillow | makhaddah | مَخَدَّه |

---

vault: قَبْو - arch: قَوْس - cellar: قَبْو لِلْمُؤَن - chair: كُرسي - bed: تَخْت (سَرير)
ashtray: مَنْفَضَة سجائِر

| | | |
|---|---|---|
| library | maktabah | مَكْتَبة |
| kitchen | maṭbakh | مَطْبَخ |
| lift | maṣ̊aad | مَصْعَد |
| chimney | madkhanah | مَدْخَنَه |
| stove | madfaảh | مَدْفَأه |
| apartment | maskan- (shaqqah) | مَسْكَن (شَقَّه) |
| pipe | māsurah | ماسورَه |
| shutter | meṣrā̊ shobbāk (darfah) | مِصْراع شُبّاك (دَرْفه) |
| fountain | nāfurah | نافورَه |

# 63 At The Book-shop

# في المكتبة 63

| | | |
|---|---|---|
| At the Bookshop | fe lmaktabah | في المَكْتَبَةْ |
| ink | ḥebr | حِبْر |
| ink bottle | qanninat ḥebr | قَنّينَةْ حِبر |
| copy-book | daftar | دَفْتَر |
| handwriting | khaṭṭ | خَطّ |
| poetry | sheʿr | شِعْر |
| chalk | ṭabshur | طَبْشور |
| dictionary | qāmus | قاموس |
| fountain pen | qalam ḥebr sāʾel | قَلَم حِبْر سائِل |
| story | qeṣṣah | قِصَّه |
| poems | qaṣāʾed ʾashʿār | قَصائِد أشْعار |
| pen | qalam ḥebr | قَلَم حِبْر |
| pencil | qalam raṣāṣ | قَلَم رَصاص |
| book | ketāb | كِتاب |
| history book | ketāb tārikh | كِتاب تاريخ |

---

perforator: خَرّامَة - pins : دَبابيس - postcard: بِطاقَة مُعايَدة - map: خَريطَة

atlas: أطْلَس (مُصَوَّر جَغرافي) - clips: مشابك للأوراق - shelves: رُفوف

mathematics: رِياضِيّات - algebra: جَبْر - biology: عِلْمُ الأحْياء

| | | |
|---|---|---|
| geography book | ketāb jaghrāfeyah | كِتاب جَغْرافيَه |
| arithmetic book | ketāb ḥesāb | كِتاب حساب |
| science book | kētab ảolum | كِتاب عُلوم |
| reading book | ketāb qerāʾ h | كِتاب قِراءَه |
| grammar book | ketāb qawāảed | كِتاب قَواعِد |
| chemistry book | ketāb kimyāʾ | كِتاب كيمياء |
| geometry book | ketāb handasah | كِتاب هَنْدَسه |
| globe | korah ảrḍeyyah | كُرَة أرْضِيَّةْ |
| blackboard | lawḥ ảswad | لَوْح أسْوَد |
| language | loghah | لُغَةْ |
| ink-pot | maḥbarah | مَحْبَره |
| ruler | masṭarah | مَسْطَرة |
| india-rubber | memḥāh | مِمْحاه |
| duster | massāḥat lawḥ | مَسّاحَة لَوْح |
| stapler | kabbāsah | كَبّاسَه |
| envelope | moghallaf | مُغَلَّف |
| plotting-paper | nashshāf | نَشَّاف |
| paper-ream | māảun waraq | ماعون وَرَق |

---

set-square: مُثَلَّث - perforator: مِنْقَله - compass: بُوصَله - compasses: فِرْجار

agenda: مفكِّرَه (note - book).

# 64 Metals — المعادن 64

| | | |
|---|---|---|
| metals | ảlmaʿāden | المعَادن |
| platinum | blātin | بْلاتينَ * |
| bronze | bronz | برونْز |
| gun-powder | bārud | بارود |
| tin | tanak | تَنَك |
| iron | ḥadid | حَديد |
| gold | dhahab | ذَهَب * |
| lead | raṣāṣ | رَصاص |
| mercury | zẻbaq | زِئْبَق |
| pitch | zeft | زِفْت |
| silver | feḍḍah | فِضَّه* |
| steel | fuladh | فولاذ |
| solder | qaṣdir | قَصْدير |
| sulphur | kebrit | كِبْريت |
| nickle | nekel | نيكِل |
| copper | noḥās ảḥmar | نُحاس أحْمَر |
| brass | naḥās ảṣfar | نُحاس أصْفَر |

*see article 54

# 65 Professions

# 65 المِهَن

| | | |
|---|---|---|
| professions | ảlmehan | أَلْمِهَن |
| cobbler | ẻskāfi | إسكافي |
| brick-layer, mason | bannāʾ | بَنَّاء |
| gardener | bostāni | بُسْتاني |
| merchant | tājer | تاجِر |
| surgeon | jarrāḥ | جَرَّاح |
| jeweller | jawharji | جَوْهَرْجي |
| guard | ḥares | حارِس |
| black-smith | ḥaddād | حَدّاد |
| plough-man | ḥarrāth | حَرّاث |
| barber | ḥallāq | حَلاّق |
| baker | khabbāz | خَبّاز |
| calligrapher | khaṭṭāṭ | خَطّاط |
| orator | khaṭib | خَطيب |
| tailor | khayyāṭ | خَيّاط |
| tanner | dabbāgh | دَبّاغ |
| painter | dahhān | دَهّان |
| draughts man | rassām | رَسّام |

| | | |
|---|---|---|
| shepherd | rāˁen | راع |
| farmer | zarrāˁ | زَرّاع |
| driver | sāˀeq | سائِق |
| watch-maker | sāˁāti | ساعاتي |
| broker | semsār | سِمْسار |
| grocer | sammān | سَمّان |
| poet | shāˁer | شاعِر |
| gold-smith | ṣāˀegh | صائِغ |
| shoe-maker | ṣāneˁ aḥdheyah | صانِع أحْذِيَة |
| banker, money-changer | ṣarrāf | صَرَّاف |
| pharmacist, chemist | ṣaydali | صَيْدَلي |
| fisher-man | ṣayyād samak | صَيَّاد سَمَك |
| doctor | ṭabib | طَبيب |
| dentist | ṭabib ˀasnān | طَبيب أسْنان |
| veterinary | ṭabib bayṭari | طَبيب بَيْطَري |
| oculist | ṭabib ˁoyun | طَبيب عُيون |
| cook | ṭāhen (ˁaachchi) | طاه (عَشّي) |
| miller | ṭaḥḥān | طَحّان |

---

Journalist: صَحَفي - dyer: صَبّاغ - foreman: رئيس عُمّال - dancer: رَقّاصه
photographer: مُصَوِّر - editor: مُحَرِّر

| | | |
|---|---|---|
| porter | ḥammāl | حَمَّال |
| apothecary | ʿaaṭṭar | عَطّار |
| artist | fannān | فَنّان |
| judge | qāḍen | قاضٍ |
| writer | kāteb | كاتِب |
| butcher | laḥḥām (jazzār) | لحَّام (جزّار) |
| lawyer,advocate | moḥāmen | مُحامٍ |
| accountant | moḥāseb | مُحاسِب |
| book-binder | mojalled kotob | مُجَلِّد كُتُب |
| teacher | moʿallem | مُعَلِّم |
| singer | moghanni | مُغَنّي |
| engineer | mohandes | مُهَنْدِس |
| actor | momaththel | مُمَثِّل |
| musician | musiqi | موسيقي |
| architect | mohandes meʿmāri | مُهَنْدِس مِعْماري |
| sculptor | naḥḥāt | نَحّات |
| carpenter | najjār | نَجّار |

# Hiring a Room اسْتِئْجار غُرْفَة



Hiring a room. ẻstẻjār ghorfah إستِئجار غُرْفَه .

I want to hire a two-bed room. أريدُ أنْ أسْتَأْجِرَ غُرْفَةً بِسَرِيرَيْن .

ỏrido ản ảstảjera ghorfatan be sarirayn

I want it to be high and for the view. أريدُها أنْ تكونَ عالِيَةً ومُشْرِفَه.

ỏridohā ản takuna ẩāleyatan wamoshrefah,

And to be away from the noise. وأنْ تكونَ بَعَيدَةً عَن الضَّجه .

waản takuna baẩidatan ẩane ḍdajjah.

I'll see what is available. سَأرى ما هُوَ مُتَوَفِّر.

saảrā mā howa motawaffer

Does the room have T.V.? هَلْ في الغُرْفَةِ تِلِفِزْيون؟

hal fe lghorfate telfezyun?

I want it for one week only. أُريدُها لِأُسْبوعٍ واحِدٍ فَقَطْ.

ỏridoha leỏsbuẩen wāḥeden faqaṭ.

---

hire: أسْتَأْجِر - bed: سَرِير - high: عالِيَة - (for the) view: مُشْرِفَة : مَنْظَر - away: بَعِيدَة

noise: ضَجّة - available: مُتَوَفِّر - week: أُسْبوع - weekly: أُسْبوعي - rates: أجُور

payment: الدَّفع - in advance: سَلَفًا - agreed: إتَّفَقْنا - have: عِنْدكَ، ولَدَيْك

identification: تَعْريف

What are your weekly rates? ما هِيَ الأُجورُ الأُسْبوعِيَّةْ؟

mā heya l ̉ojuro l ̉osbuʿaeyyah?

Here is a list of our prices. ها هِيَ قائِمَةٌ بِأَسْعارِنا .

hā heya qāʾematon beʾasʿārena.

Our policy is payment in advance. سِياسَتُنا الدَّفْعُ سَلَفًا .

seyāsatonā ddafʿo salafan.

Ok. Agreed. ḥasanan ʾettafaqnā. حَسَنًا . إتَّفَقْنا.

Do you have identifications? هَلْ لَدَيْكَ أَوْراقْ تَعريْف؟

hal ladayka ʾawrāq taʿarif?

Yes, my passport and a driving licence. نَعَمْ، جَوازْ سَفَري ورُخْصَةُ سِواقَةْ .

naʿam, jawāz safari warokhṣato sewāqah.

Wait for a moment, please. إنْتَظِر لَحْظَةً مِنْ فَضْلِك .

ʾentaḍher laḥḍhatan men faḍlek

I'll call the bell-boy for your luggage. سَأَدْعو الخادِمَ لِيَحْمِلَ أغْراضَك .

saʾadʿu lkhādema leyaḥmela ʾaghrāḍak.

---

passport: جَواز سَفَر - driving: سِواقَةْ - licence: رُخْصَةْ
wait for: إنْتَظِر - moment: لَحْظَهْ
call: أَدْعو - bell-boy: خادِم

# 67 Trade — التِّجارَة 67

| | | |
|---|---|---|
| trade | ảttejārah | التِّجارَة |
| agreement | ẻttefāq | إتّفاق |
| monopoly | ẻḥtekar | إحْتِكار |
| sending | ẻrsāl | إرْسال |
| consumption | ẻstehlāk | إسْتِهْلاك |
| importation | ẻstirād | إسْتيراد |
| receipt | ẻstelām-Waṣl | إسْتلام – وَصْل |
| business | ảshghāl | أَشْغال |
| failure-bankruptcy | ẻflās | إفْلاس |
| production | ẻntāj | إنْتاج |
| notice | ẻndhār | إنْذار |
| seller-merchant | bāẻả | بائِع |
| goods | beḍāảah | بِضاعَه |
| fixed price | thaman maḥdud | ثَمَن مَحْدود |
| by whole sale | beljomlah | بالجُمْلَةْ |
| loss | khasārah | خَسارَه |

---

consignment: إرْساليِّة - signature: إمْضاء - deposit: عَربون، تأمين - tariff: تَعْرِفَة

reduction: تنَزْيل - producer: مُنْتِج - by retail: بالمُفَرَّق

| | | |
|---|---|---|
| debt | dayn | دَيْن |
| gain, benefit | rebḥ | ربْح |
| balance | raṣid | رَصيد |
| packet | razmah | رَزْمَه |
| customer | zabun | زَبون |
| commissioner-broker | semsār | سِمْسار |
| share | sahm-ḥeṣṣah | سَهْم – حِصَّةْ |
| document | sanad | سَنَد |
| partner | sharik | شَريك |
| purchase | sherāɔ | شراء |
| company-society | sharekah | شَركَه |
| quality | ṣenf | صِنْف |
| net | ṣāfen | صاف |
| exchange | ṣerāfah | صِرافَه |
| package-parcel | ṭard | طَرْد |
| order | ṭalabeyyah | طَلَبيَّةْ |
| paper money | ̊aemlah waraqeyyah | عِمْلَه ورَقيَّة |
| coin | ̊aemlah maådaneyyah | عِمْلَه مَعْدَنيّةْ |
| interest | fāɔedah | فائدَه |

---

export:صادر - sender: مُرْسِل - import: وارد - importer: مُوَرِّد - exporter: مُصَدِّر

immovable: غَيْر مَنْقولَة - agent:وكيل - transaction:صَفْقَة، مُعامَلة تجاريَّة

| | | |
|---|---|---|
| occasion | forṣah | فُرْصَه |
| value | qimah | قيمَةْ |
| instal (1) ment | qesṭ | قِسْط |
| gross | qāẻm | قائِم |
| quantity | kammeyyah | كَمِيَّةْ |
| bill | kombyālah - fāturat ḥesāb | كُمْبيالَة - فاتورَة حِساب |
| pattern | masṭarah - ʿaayyenah | مَسْطَرَهْ - عَيّنَه |
| accountant | moḥāseb | مُحاسِب |
| contractor | moqāwel | مُقاوِل |
| movable | manqulah | مَنْقوله |
| project | mashruʿ | مَشْروع |
| expenses | nafaqāt | نَفقَات |
| cash | naqdan | نَقْداً |

| | | |
|---|---|---|
| Nature | åṭṭabiååah | الطَّبيعَة |
| earth | årḍ | أرْض |
| region | èqlim | إقلْيم |
| horizon | ỏfoq | أفُقُ |
| lightning | barq | بَرْق |
| sea | baḥr | بَحْر |
| lake | boḥayrah | بُحَيْرَة |
| volcano | borkān | بُرْكان |
| cold | bard - bāred | بَرْد – بارِد |
| soil | torāb | تُراب |
| hill | tallah | تَلةّ |
| snow | thalj | ثَلجْ |
| harbour | thaghr-minā | ثَغْر–ميناء |
| mountain | jabal | جَبَل |
| island | jazirah | جَزيرة |
| ice | jalid | جَليد |
| south | janub | جَنوب |

---

ebb: جَزْر jazr

| | | |
|---|---|---|
| atmosphere | jaww | جَوّ |
| stone | ḥajar | حَجَر |
| pebbles | ḥaṣā | حَصَى |
| hot | ḥārr | حارّ |
| bay | khalij | خَليج |
| eclipse | khosuf-kosuf | خُسوف-كُسوف |
| equator | khaṭṭe l ʾestewāʾ | خَطّ الإسْتِواء |
| smoke | dokhān | دُخان |
| thunder | raʿad | رَعْد |
| moisture | roṭubah | رُطوبَه |
| sand | raml | رَمْل |
| wind | riḥ | ريح |
| earthquake | zelzāl | زلزال |
| storm | zawbaʿah | زَوْبَعه |
| coast | sāḥel | ساحِل |
| plain | sahl | سَهْل |
| sea-shore | shāṭiʾ | شاطِئ |
| east | sharq | شَرْق |
| spark | sharārah | شَرارَةْ |
| north | shamāl | شَمال |

---

tide: مدّ madd

| | | |
|---|---|---|
| sun | shams | شَمْس |
| thunderbolt | ṣāʿeqah | صاعِقَةْ |
| desert | ṣaḥrāʾ | صَحْراء |
| rock | ṣakhrah | صَخْرَةْ |
| weather | ṭaqs | طَقْس |
| flood | ṭufān | طوفان |
| dark | ḍhalām- moḍhlem | ظَلام – مُظْلِم |
| shade | ḍhell | ظِلّ |
| storm | ʿāṣefah | عاصِفَةْ |
| dust | ghobār | غُبار |
| west | gharb | غَرْب |
| cloud | ghaymah-saḥābah | غَيْمة – سَحابَه |
| continent | qārrah | قارَّه |
| pole | qoṭb | قُطْب |
| moon | qamar | قَمَر |
| top | qemmah | قِمَّه |
| canal | qanāh | قَناه |
| rainbow | qaws qozaḥ | قَوْس قُزَح |
| universe | ʾalkawn | أَلْكَوْن |
| water | māʾ | ماء |
| ocean | moḥiṭ | مُحيط |
| zone | manṭeqah | مَنْطِقَهْ |

| | | |
|---|---|---|
| climate | monākh | مُناخ |
| wave | mawjah | مَوْجَه |
| fire | nār | نار |
| spring | nabˁ | نَبْع |
| star | najm | نَجْم |
| river | nahr | نَهْر |
| light | nur | نور |
| air | hawāˀ | هَواء |
| valley | wādi | وادي |
| mud | waḥl | وَحْل |
| oasis | wāḥah | واحَةْ |

# 69 Trees     الأَشْجار 69

| | | |
|---|---|---|
| trees | ảlảshjār | الأَشْجار |
| pear tree | shajarat ẻjaṣ | شَجَرة إجاص |
| orange tree | shajarat bortoqāl | شَجَرة بُرْتُقال |
| oak tree | shajarat balluṭ | شَجَرة بَلّوط |
| palm tree | shajarat balaḥ | شَجَرة بَلَح |
| hazelnut tree | shajarat bondoq | شَجَرة بُنْدُق |
| apple tree | shajarat toffāḥ | شَجَرة تُفّاح |
| mulberry tree | shajarat tut | شَجَرة توت |
| fig tree | shajarat tin | شَجَرة تين |
| walnut tree | shajarat jaws | شَجَرة جَوْز |
| nutmeg tree | shajarat jawsat ảṭṭib | شَجَرة جَوْز الطِّيب |
| coconut tree | shajarat jawz ảlhend | شَجَرة جَوْز الهِنْد |
| poplar tree | shajarat ḥur | شَجَرة حَوْر |
| carob tree | shajarat kharnub | شَجَرة خَرْنوب |

---

some of these trees are fruit trees mentioned in article number 47.

lemon tree شَجَرة حامِض ḥāmeḍ

plum tree — shajarat khawkh — شَجَرة خَوْخ

cane tree — shajarat khayzarān — شَجَرة خَيْزَران

elm tree — shajarat dardār — شَجَرة دَرْدار

peach tree — shajarat dorrāq — شَجَرة دُرّاق

pomegranate tree — shajarat rommān — شَجَرة رُمّان

beech tree — shajarat zān — شَجَرة زان

olive tree — shajarat zaytoun — شَجَرة زَيْتون

cypress tree — shajarat sarw — شَجَرة سَرْو

quince tree — shajarat safarjal — شَجَرة سَفَرْجَل

willow tree — shajarat ṣofṣāf — شَجَرة صُفْصاف

jujube tree — shajarat ʿennāb — شَجَرة عنّاب

pistachio tree — shajarat fostoq — شَجَرة فُسْتُق

chestnut tree — shajarat kastanāʾ — شَجَرة كَسْتَناء

vine tree — karmah (ʿenab) — كَرمْه (عنَب)

almond tree — shajarat lawz — شَجَرة لَوْز

banana tree — shajarat mawz — شَجَرة مَوْز

apricot tree — shajarat moshmosh — شَجَرة مُشْمُش

---

trunk: جذع الشَّجَرة :jedhʿ - cluster: عُنْقود ʿonqud - branch: غُصْن ghoṣn
stalk: ساق sāq - bark: قِشْرَة qeshrah

# 70 Kitchen Ware أدَواتُ المَطْبَخ

| | | |
|---|---|---|
| pitcher | ẻbriq | إبْريق |
| tea - pot | ẻbriq shāy | إبريق شاي |
| coffee-pot | ẻbriq qahwah | إبريق قَهْوَة |
| milk-jug | ẻbriq ḥalib | إبريق حَليب |
| refrigerator | barrād | بَرّاد |
| barrel | barmil | بَرْميل |
| cork-screw | barrimah | بَرّيمَة (فَتّاحة عِلْبَةْ) |
| sugar-bowl | sokkareyyah | سُكَّرِيَّة |
| knife | sekkinah | سِكّينَةْ |
| basket | sallah | سَلَّة |
| roller | shubak | شوبْك |
| fork | shawkah | شَوْكَة |
| dish-plate | ṣaḥn | صَحْن |
| tray | ṣineyyah | صينِيَّة |
| saucer | ṣaḥn fenjān | صَحْن فِنْجان |
| mill | ṭāḥunah | طاحونَه |
| cooking pan | ṭanjarah | طَنْجَرة |
| kettle | ghallayah | غَلاَّيَة |
| lid | gheṭā' | غِطاء |

utensil: وِعاء، إناء weʿāʾ , ẻnāʾ

| | | |
|---|---|---|
| oven | forn | فُرْن |
| cork | fallin | فِلّين |
| cup | fenjān | فنْجان |
| tea-cup | fenjān shāy | فِنْجان شاي |
| bottle | qanninah | قَنّينَة |
| pot | qedr | قِدْر |
| cage | qafaṣ | قَفَص |
| funnel | qemaʕ | قِمع |
| glass | kobbāyah | كُبّايَةْ |
| pepper-box | mabharah | مَبْهَره |
| filter | meṣfāh | مِصْفاه |
| kitchen | maṭbakh | مَطْبَخ |
| frying-pan | maqlā | مَقْلى |
| broom | meknasah | مِكْنَسةْ |
| spoon | melʕaqah | مِلْعَقَةْ |
| tea-spoon | melʕaqat shāy | مِلعقة شاي |
| tongs | malqaṭ | مَلْقَط |
| sieve | monkhol | مُنْخُل |
| ashtray | manfaḍah | مَنْفَضهْ |

---

ironer: مَكْوى makwā

# 71 Insects and Reptiles

# الحشَرات والزَّواحِف 71

| | | |
|---|---|---|
| insects and reptiles | ảlḥasharāt wazzawāḥef | الحَشَرات والزَّواحِف |
| viper | ảfʿā sāmmah | أفْعى سَامَّة |
| flea | borghuth | بُرْغوث |
| mosquito | barghashah | بَرْغشَه-بَعوضه |
| bug | baqqah | بَقّة |
| serpent | thoʿbān | ثُعبان |
| locust | jarādah | جَرادَه |
| grasshopper | jondob | جُنْدُب |
| snake | ḥayyah | حَيّه |
| chameleon | ḥerbāʾ | حِرْباء |
| insect | ḥasharah | حَشَره |
| beetle | khonfosah | خُنْفُسَه |
| worm | dudah | دودَه |
| wasp | dabbur | دَبُّور |
| caterpillar | dudat shajar | دودَة شَجَر |
| silkworm | dudat qazz | دودَة قَزّ |
| fly | dhobābah | ذُبابَه |
| reptile | zāḥefah | زاحِفَهْ |

| | | |
|---|---|---|
| drone | dhakaro nnaḥl | ذَكَر النَّحْل |
| lizard | saḥleyyah | سَحْلِيَّه |
| cricket | ṣorṣur | صُرْصور |
| moth | ʿaethth | عِثّ |
| scorpion | ʿaaqrab | عَقْرَب |
| spider | ʿaankabut | عَنْكَبوت |
| butterfly | farāshah | فَراشَه |
| louse | qamlah | قَمْلَه |
| bee | naḥlah | نَحْلَه |
| ant | namlah | نَمْلَه |

---

poison: سُمّ somm - venomous: سامّ sāmm - wing: جَناح janāḥ - leg: رِجْل rejl

legs: أرْجُل ʾarjol - antidote: مُضادّ للسُّم moḍad lessom (تِرْياق)

# 72 Measurements المقاييس 72

| | | |
|---|---|---|
| measurements | ảlmaqāyis | المَقاييس |
| ounce | ỏqeyyah | أوُقيّة (28, 35 غرام) |
| inch | ẻnsh | إِنْش - بوصه 2,54 سم |
| dozen | dazzinah | دَزّينَه ( 12 وحدة) |
| cubit | dherāả | ذِراع (إنْش 18 ) |
| span | shebr | شِبْر (9 إنش) |
| ton | ṭonn | طُنّ (1000 كيلو) |
| gram | ghrām | غْرام |
| acre | faddān | فَدّان (4840 يارد مربع) |
| league | farsakh | فَرْسَخ (ميل 2,4-4.6 ) |
| fathom | qāmah | قامَه (6 قدم) |
| foot | qadam | قَدَم (1/3 يارده) = ٥ ، ٣٠ سم |
| kilogram | kilo ghrām | كيلو غْرام (1000 غرام ) |
| gross | kruz | كْروز (12 دزينه) |
| pound | librah | لِيْبَره (453 غرام) |

---

fathom: used for measuring the depth of water.

weight: وَزْن wazn - measure: مِقْياس meqyas

| | | |
|---|---|---|
| meter | metr | مِتْر |
| square meter | metr morabbaˁ | مِتْر مُرَبَّع |
| cubic meter | metr mokaˁˁab | مِتْر مُكَعَّب |
| hectare | hektār | هِكْتار (10000 م$^2$) |
| yard | yārdah | يارْدَه (91.44 سم) |

| invitations | ảddaảwāt | الدَّعْوات |
|---|---|---|

I was delighted to receive your letter. سُرِرْتُ لأنْ أستَلِمَ رِسالَتك .

sorerto leản ảstalema resālatak.

How are you all? كَيْفَ حالكُمْ جَميعًا؟

kayfa ḥālokom jamiảan?

We are all well . نَحْنُ جَميعًا بِخَيْر .

naḥno jamiảan bekhayr.

We hope you are well, too . نَأمَلُ أنْ تَكونوا بِخَيْر أيضًا .

naảmal ản takunu bekhayr ảyḍan.

We are busy these days. نَحْنُ مَشْغولونْ هَذِهِ الأيّام .

naḥno mashghulun hādhehe lảyyām.

Next Sunday is our son's wedding. الأحَدُ القادِمْ حَفْلَةْ زَواجْ وَلَدِنا .

ảl ảḥado lqādem ḥaflat zawaj waladenā.

---

delight: يَسُرّ yasorr - well: بخَيْر -busy: مَشْغول - hope: نأمل - too: أيضًا -days: أيّام -
next: القادِم - invite: نَدْعو - please: يَسُرّ - please: نَرْجو - inform: يُخبِر ، يُعلِم
declined: إعْتَذَرْتُم

We are pleased to invite you for lunch. يَسُرُّنا أنْ نَدْعوكُمْ لِزِيارَتِنا عَلَى الغَداء .

yasorronā ̉an nad̉ukom lezeyāratenā ̉ala lghadā̉

Please inform us if you declined . نَرْجو أنْ تُخْبِرونا إذا اعْتَذَرْتُم عَنِ الحُضور .

narju ̉an tokhberunā ̉edhā ̉atadhartom ̉aane lḥoḍur.

Good-bye. إلى الِّلقــاء .

̉ela lleqā̉

# Making An Apology الإعــــــتِـــــــذار



Making an Apology ālẻåtedhār الإعْتِذار

Hello Ahmad, tell me how to apologize. هالو أحْمَد، أخبِرْني كَيْفَ أعتَذِر.

halu åḥmad, åkhberni kayfa åǻtadher.

What do I say when I am late? ماذا أقولُ عِنْدَما أتأخَّر؟

mādhā åqulo ǻendamā åtåkhkhar?

Say: I am sorry I am late. قُلْ: أنا آسِف أنِّي متَأخِّر.

qol ånā ā sef ånni motåkhkher.

or, say: I am very sorry I am late. أوْ، قُلْ: أنا آسِف جِدّاً أنّي مُتأخِّر.

åw, qol: ånā āsef jeddan ånni motåkhkher.

How to ask to put off an appointment? كَيْفَ أطْلُبُ تَأجيلَ مَوْعِد؟

kayfa åṭlobo taåjila mawǻed?

**Say**: Would you mind to put off ... for next week?

qol: hal tomāneǻ ån toåjjel ... le lösbuǻe lqādem?

قُلْ: هَلْ تُمانِعْ أنْ تُؤَجِّلْ... لِلأسْبوعِ القادِم؟

Don't say: sorry. I can't. - لا تَقُلْ: آسِف. أنا لا أقْدِر.

lā taqol āsef. ånā lā åqder.

Say: I'm afraid I can't. - قُلْ: أخْشَى أنْ لا أقْدِر .

qol: ảkhshā ản lā ảqder.

- إذا أرَدْتَ أنْ تَسْأَلْ عَنِ الطَّرِيق إلى مَصْرَف . . .

If you want to ask about the way to... bank

ẻdhā ảradta ản tasảl a̔ne ṭṭariq ẻlā maṣraf ....

قُلْ: عَفْوًا (أعْذُرْني)، هَلْ تَسْتَطيعُ أنْ تُخْبِرَني عَنِ الطَّرِيْق لِمَصْرف. . .

Say: excuse me, can you tell me the way to...bank?

qol: ỏa̔dhorni, hal tastaṭia̔o ản tokhberani a̔ne ṭṭarik lemasraf...

قُلْ: عَفْوًا، عِنْدما تُخْطِىءْ مَعْ إنْسانٍ ما..

Say: excuse me, when you do wrong to somebody .

qol a̔afwan, a̔endamā tokhṭẻ maa̔ ẻnsānen mā.

# 75 State — الدَّوْلَة 75

| | | |
|---|---|---|
| Independence | ẻsteqlāl | إِسْتِقْلال |
| mandate | ẻntedāb | إِنْتِداب |
| election | ẻntekhāb | إِنْتِخاب |
| parliament | bărlamān | بَرْلَمان |
| voting | taṣwit | تَصْويت |
| republic | jomhureyyah | جُمْهورِيَّةْ |
| session | jalsah | جَلْسَةْ |
| autonomy | ḥokm dhāti | حُكْم ذاتِيّ |
| protection | ḥemayah | حِمَايَةْ |
| party | ḥezb | حِزْب |
| constitution | dostur | دُستور |
| president | raẻis jomhureyyah | رَئيس جُمْهورِيَّةْ |
| authority | solṭah | سُلْطَةْ |
| embassy | safārah | سَفارَه |
| ambassador | safir | سَفير |
| capital | ʿāāṣemah | عاصِمَهْ |
| consulate | qonṣoleyyah | قُنْصُلِيَّه |
| consul | qonṣol | قُنْصُل |
| king | malek | مَلِك |

| | | |
|---|---|---|
| kingdom | mamlakah | مَمْلَكَةْ |
| independent | mostaqell | مُسْتَقِلّ |
| candidate | morashshaḥ | مُرَشَّح |
| conference | mo̓tamar | مُؤْتَمر |
| opposition | mo̔āraḍah | مُعارَضَةْ |
| vice | nāe̓b | نَائِب |
| minister | wazir | وَزِير |
| Prime Minister | wazir a̓wwal - ra̓es wazārah | وَزِير أوَّل - رئيس وَزارَهْ |
| Ministry | wāzarah | وَزارَهْ |
| Ministry of Public Works | wazārat a̓la̓shghāl | وَزارَة الأشْغال |
| Ministry of Education | wazarat a̓ttarbeyah | وَزارَة التَّربيَهْ |
| Ministry of Foreign Affairs | wazarat a̓lkhārejeyyah | وَزارَة الخارجيّه |
| Ministry of Interior | wazarat a̓ddākheleyyah | وَزارَة الدَّاخِلِيَّهْ |
| Ministry of Health | wazarat a̓ṣṣeḥḥah | وَزارَة الصِّحَّهْ |
| Ministry of Justice | wazarat a̓la̔adleyyah | وَزارَة العَدْلِيَّهْ |
| Ministry of Finance | wazarat a̓lmāleyyah | وَزارَة الماليَّهْ |
| Ministry of Defence | wazarat a̓ddefāa̔ | وَزارَة الدِّفاع |
| taxes | ḍarāe̓b | ضَرائِب |
| Public Security | a̓mn a̔āmm | أَمْن عامّ |
| director - general | modir a̔āmm | مُدير عامّ |
| inspector | mofattesh | مُفَتِّش |
| director | modir | مُدير |
| municipality | baladeyyah | بَلَدِيَّهْ |
| mayor | raēis baladeyyah | رَئيس بَلَدِيَّهْ |

# 76 Law Terms

# 76 إصْطِلاحات حُقُوقِيَّة

| | | |
|---|---|---|
| claim | ẻddeʿāʾ | إدّعاء |
| confession | ẻqrār | إقْرار |
| appeal | ẻstẻnāf | إسْتِئْناف |
| revision | ẻʿādah | إعادَة |
| decleration | ẻfādah | إفادَة |
| denial | ẻnkār | إنْكار |
| lease | ẻijār | إيجار |
| provisional | ẻḥteyāṭi | إحْتِياطي |
| principal | ảṣil | أصِيل |
| protestation | ẻḥtejāj | إحْتِجاج |
| proof | borhān | بُرْهان |
| arbitration | taḥkim | تَحْكيم |
| ratification | taṣdiq | تَصْديق |
| confirmation | tảyid | تَأْييد |
| contradiction | tanaqoḍ | تَناقُض |
| appropriation | tamallok | تَمَلُّك |
| adjournment | tảjil | تَأْجيل |
| executive | tanfidhi | تَنْفيذي |
| compensation | taʿawiḍ | تَعْويض |

| | | |
|---|---|---|
| signification | tabligh | تَبْليغ |
| criminal | jenāʾei | جِنائي |
| judgement | ḥokm - qaḍāʾ | حُكْم – قَضاء |
| share | ḥeṣṣah | حِصّه |
| seizure | ḥajz | حَجْز |
| right | ḥaq | حَقّ |
| argument | ḥojjah | حُجَّه |
| defence | defāʿ | دِفاع |
| indication | dalil | دَليل |
| cause | daʿwa | دَعْوى |
| propaganda | deʿāyah | دِعَايَةْ |
| rejection | radd - rafḍ | رَدّ – رَفْض |
| mortgage | rahn | رَهْن |
| pretext | zaʿm | زَعْم |
| document | sanad | سَنَد |
| evidence | shahādah | شَهادَه |
| witness | shāhed | شاهِد |
| personal | shakhṣei | شَخْصيّ |
| damage | ḍarar | ضَرَر |
| pretension | ṭalab | طَلَب |
| public | ʿāmm | عَامّ |
| invalidation | faskh | فَسْخ |

| | | |
|---|---|---|
| cause | qaḍeyyah | قَضيّة |
| judiciary | qaḍāʾei | قَضائيّ |
| guaranty | kafālah | كَفالَه |
| guarantor | kafil | كَفيل |
| verification | kashf | كَشْف |
| conclusion | lāʾeḥah - qararḥokm | لائِحَه - قَرارحُكْم |
| title | laqab | لَقَب |
| matter | māddah | مادّة |
| procés verbal | maḥḍar | مَحْضَر |
| acquired | moktasab | مُكْتَسَب |
| remuneration | mokāfaʾah | مُكافَاه |
| lessor | moʾajjer | مُؤَجِّر |
| lessee - tenant | mostaʾjer | مُسْتَأجِر |
| bid | mazād | مَزاد |
| plaintiff | moddaʿi | مُدَّعي |
| defendant | moddaʿā ʿalayh | مُدَّعى عَلَيْه |
| appellant | mostaʾnef | مُسْتَأنِف |
| appellee | mostaʾnaf ʿalayh | مُسْتَأنف عَلَيْه |
| civil | madani | مَدَنّي |
| alliance | moḥālafah | مُحالَفة |
| oath | yamin | يَمين |
| perjury | shahādat zur | شَهادَة زور |

# 77 Disciplinary Terms

# 77 اصطلاحات جَزائِيَّة

| | | |
|---|---|---|
| accusation | ȅttehām | إتِّهام |
| arrest | ȅa̔teqāl | إعْتِقال |
| conviction | ȅdānah | إدانَه |
| forced residence | ȅqāmah jabreyyah | إقامَهْ جَبْرِيَّه |
| deportation | ȅba̔ād | إبْعاد |
| suspicion | ȅshtebāh | إشْتِباه |
| correction | ȅṣlāḥ | إصْلاح |
| security | ȁmn | أَمْنْ |
| innocence | baraȁh | بَراءَه |
| innocent | bariˀ | بَريء |
| inculpation - charge | tohmah | تُهْمَهْ |
| search - detection | taḥarri | تَحَرِّي |
| inquiry | taḥqiq | تَحْقيق |
| detention | tawqif | تَوْقيف |
| extradition | taslim ȁlmojremin | تَسْليم المُجْرِمين |
| imprisonment | ḥabs | حَبْس |
| judgment | ḥokm | حُكْم |

| | | |
|---|---|---|
| condemned | maḥkum | مَحْكوم |
| condemned to death | maḥkum ẻa̔dām | مَحْكوم إعْدام |
| penal servitude | maḥkum ảshghāl shāqqah | مَحْكوم أشغْال شاقّة |
| sentenced for life | maḥkum mỏabbad | مَحْكوم مُؤبَّد |
| amnesty | a̔afw | عَفْو |
| penalty | a̔oqubah | عُقُوبَه |
| fine | gharāmah | غَرامَه |
| guilty | modhneb | مُذْنِب |
| suspected | mashbuh | مَشْبوه |
| warrant | modhakkarah | مُذَكَّره |
| curfew | mana̔ tajawwol | مَنْع تَجَوُّل |
| detained | mawquf | مَوْقوف |
| plaint | shakwā | شَكْوى |
| plaintiff | moshtaki | مُشْتَكِي |

# 78 Proverbs

# أمْـــــــثـــــال 78

Proverbs are the fruit of long experience. They give us a piece of wisdom. It is important to notice that sometimes the Arabic Proverb differs a little from the English Proverb literally.

Proverbs are helpful especially in conversation since they are short and eloquent. Arabic proverbs are in thousands; I hope to have been successful in choosing some few proverbs that may enjoy the reader.

Here are some proverbs:

1 . الأعمالُ خَيْرٌ مِنَ الأقْوال . — ảl ảamālo khayron mena lảqwāl.

1. Acts speak louder than words.

2 . إنَّ معَ العُسْرِ يُسْراً . — ẻnna maảa lảosre yosran.

2. After a storm comes sun shine (fair weather).

This is said to calm down a person who is in difficulty – عُسْر

and to let him feel that after the difficulty there will be ease – يُسْر

---

union : إتِّحاد – strength : قُوَّة – acts : أعْمال – words : أقْوال – difficulty : عُسْر – ease : يُسْر

fire : نار – strike : إضْرِب – iron : حديد – hot : ساخِن ، حامي – matters : أمور – ends : خَواتِم

ȇstajāra mena rramḍāִ bennār. 3 . إسْتَجارَ مِنَ الرَّمْضاء بالنّار .

3. to jump out of the frying pan into the fire.

This is said about a man who was in hot land - رَمْضاء - and asked the help of some body - إسْتَجارَ - but fell in the worse - بالنّار

ȃl ȏmuro bekhawātemehā. 4. الأُمورُ بخَواتمها .

4. All is well that ends well.

We must not judge matters – ألأُمور till the ends – نهايَات، خَواتم

ȇḍreb ḥadidan ḥāmeyan . 5 . إضْربْ حَديداً حامياً .

5. Strike while the iron is hot.

ȃl ȇtteḥado qowwaton. 6 . الإتّحادُ قُوّةٌ .

6. Union is Strength.

Union: اتحاد - Strength:قوّة

ȇttaqe sharra man ȃḥsanta ȇlayh 7 . إتَّقِ شَرَّ مَنْ أحْسَنْتَ إلِيْه .

7. Beware the man who has received charity from you.

ȇdha aradta ȃn totāȃ, sal mā yostaṭāȃ 8 . إذا أردْتَ أنْ تُطاع ، سَلْ ما يُسْتَطاع

8. If you wish to be obeyed, don't ask the impossible.

ȇdhā habbat reyāḥoka faghtanemhā. 9 . إذا هبَّتْ رياحُكَ فاغتّنمْها .

9. Make hay while the sun shines.

This Arabic proverb is literally different from the English one, but the meaning is the same. It means, if the wind blows run your boat because you don't know when it stops. The same meaning has the English proverb: if you have sun shine, put the grass out in the sun to dry (to become hay), because you don't know when it will be cloudy. (note the English weather) shortly, seize the opportunity and don't waste it.

ẻnna ṯṯoyura ẩlā ảshkāleha taqaẩo. **10 . إِنَّ الطُّيورَ على أشكالِها تقَعُ .**

10. Birds of a feather flock together

Birds of the same feather fly together.

(taqaẩ) here means be together = flock

This proverb is said about good people who associate with good people, or about bad people who associate with bad people.

yoẩrafo lmar› beảqrāneh. يُعْرَفُ المَرْءُ بأَقْرانه .

is known: يُعْرَف - The person: المَرْء - by his company:بأَقْرانه

ảl ẻskāf ḥafen walḥāẻk ẩaryān. **11 . الإسْكاف حافٍ والحائِك عَرْيان .**

11. The cobbler's children (wife) are the worst shod.

undressed : عَرْيان – cobbler : إسْكاف – barefooted : حافٍ – weaver : حائِك

---

beware: إحْذَر، إتَّق - charity: إحْسان - be obeyed: تُطاع - ask: يَسأل

don't ask:لا تسأل (لا تَسَل) possible: مُمْكِن، مُسْتَطاع - get benefit of: إغْتَنِم

blew: هَبَّتْ - wind/s: رِيح / رِياح – feather: رِيشَه

ʾal ʾamānato ʾafḍalo seyāsah. 12 . الأمانَةُ أفْضَلُ سِياسَه .

12. Honesty is the best policy.

honesty : أمانه - best : الأحْسَن ، الأفْضَل - policy : سِياسَه

This is said to advise a person or to comment on some behaviour or conduct.

13 . إذا كانَ الكَلامُ مِنْ فِضّةٍ فالسُّكوتُ مِن ذَهَبْ .

ʾedhā kāna lkalāmo men feḍḍaten fassokuto men dhahab.

13. Speech is silver, silence is gold.

Speech: كَلام - silver: فِضَّه - silence: سُكوت - gold: ذَهَب

This is said to a person to be less talkative.

ʾaoṭlobe lʿaelma mena lmahde ʾela llaḥd . 14 . أُطْلُبِ العِلْمَ مِنَ المَهْدِ إلى اللَّحْد

14. Seek knowledge from the cradle to the grave.

Seek: أُطْلُب ، إبْحَث عن - Knowledge: عِلْم ، مَعْرِفه

Cradle: مَهْد ، سَرير - grave: لَحْد ، قَبْر

This means that we have to seek knowledge as long as we are alive.

15 . الأواني الفارِغَةُ تُحْدِثُ الضَّجةَ الكُبْرى .

ʾal ʾawāne lfāreghato toḥdetho ḍḍajjata lkobrā.

15. Empty vessels make the most noise.

empty: فارِغ - vessel: إناء ، وِعاء - make: يُحْدِث ، يَصْنَع - noise: ضَجّه ، صَوْت

most: الكُبْرى ، الأكْبَر ، الأكثر

This is said about an uninformed person who makes trouble to cover his ignorance .

bekolle ăors laho qorṣ. 16 . بِكُلِّ عُرْسٍ لَه قُرْص .

16. He puts his finger in too many pies.

This is said about a man who interfers in many matters that do not concern him.

Wedding, party: حَفْلة ، عُرس - cake: كَعْكَة ، قُرص - pie.

ăl barakato fi lbokur. 17 . البَركَةُ في البُكور .

17. The early bird catches the worm.

catches: يلتَقط يُمْسك - worm: دُودَه

This is said to encourage people to go early to work, because they will be successful, as the bird that flies early to the fields will find a worm to feed on.

ăttadbiro neṣfo lmaăishah. 18 . التَّدْبيرُ نِصْفُ المعِيشهْ .

18. economy entails half the livelihood.

economy: تَدْبير ، إقْتصاد - entails: يُؤَدي إلى نَتيجَة - half: نِصْف - livelihood: مَعيشَه

This proverb is to advise people who are extravagant to be economical in their expenditure.

ăljāro qabla ddār. 19 . الجارُ قَبْلَ الدَّار .

19. choose your neighbour before you choose your house.

ăl ḥasud lā yasud . 20 . الحَسود لا يَسود .

(jealous : حَسود – succeed : يَنْجَح يَسود)

20. Victory doesn't come by jealousy.

**21** . خيرُ الأمورِ الوَسَط (وَسَط : middle – خيْر : best – طُرُق ، أمُور : ways)

khayro lomure lwasaṭ.

21. The middle way is the best way.

ȁddarzato fi waqtehā towaffero tesȁan.. . **22** . الدَّرْزَةُ في وقْتِها تُوفِّرُ تسّعًا .

22. a stitch in time saves nine.

في وَقْتِها : in time – تُوَفِّر : saves – خِيَاطه ، دَرْزَه : stitch

It is advisable to sew a torn place in a shirt, for example, in time; because if you don't do that the torn place will widen and cost you much to mend it.

derhamo weqāyaten khayron men qonṭāre ȁelaj. . **23** . دِرْهَمُ وِقايَةٍ خَيْرٌ مِنْ قُنْطارِ عِلاج

23. Prevention is better than cure.

علاج : cure - (a lot of...) ، قُنْطار : quintal (a little of ...) ، دِرهم : dram

dārhem mā domta fi dārehem . **24** . دارِهِم مادُمْتَ في دارِهِم .

24. When in Rome do as the Romans do.

دارِهِم : their house – ما دُمْتَ : while you are – دارِهِم : flatter them

rȁso lḥekmate makhāfato llāh. **25** . رأسُ الحِكْمَةِ مَخافَةُ الله .

25. The fear of God is the beginning of wisdom.

(حكمه : wisdom – بدايَة ، رأس : beginning – مخافة : fear) .

ȁsserro ēdhā jāwaza lethnayne shāȁ. **26** . السرُّ إذا جاوَزَ الإِثْنَيْنِ شاعَ .

26. A secret, when known by or told to more than two people, will be (spread : شاعَ ، إِنْتَشَر) no more secret.

ảṣṣadiq ảenda ḍḍiq. **27 . الصَّديق عِنْدَ الضِّيق .**

27. A friend in need is a friend indeed.

in need: عِنْدَ الحاجَة، عِنْد الضِّيق - indeed: حقًّا = (really)

A real and faithful friend is the friend who will help you when you are in a difficulty and need help.

aṣṣabro meftāḥo lfaraj. **28 . الصَّبْرُ مِفْتاحُ الفَرَج .**

28. Patience is the key to relief.

patience : الصَّبْر – key : مِفْتاح – relief : فَرَج، إسْعاف

ảttabảo yaghlebo ttaṭabboả. **29 . الطَّبْعُ يُغلِبُ التَّطَبّعُ .**

29. The leopard doesn't change its spots.

temper : طَبْع – affectation : تَطَبُّع، تَصَنُّع – dominate : يَغْلِب، يَسُود على

The man / woman who is dishonest, however he / she tries to be honest, his /her dishonesty will show up.

ảalā qadare besāṭeka modda rejlayk.. **30 . على قَدَرِ بِساطِكَ مُدَّ رِجلَيك .**

30. Cut your coat according to your cloth.

according to : على قدَر، حَسَب – carpet : بِساط – Stretch : مُدّ – legs : رِجْلَيْن

This means that we must live according to our income.

ảl ảelmo lqalilo khaṭer. **31 . العِلْمُ القَليلُ خَطِر .**

31. A little learning is a dangerous thing.

learning : عِلْم، تَعَلُّم – little : قَليل – dangerous : خَطِر

32 . عَدُوٌّ عاقِلٌ خَيْرٌ مَنْ صَديقٍ جاهِلٍ .

ٓaadowwon ٓaāqelon khayron men ṣadiqen jāhel.

32. A wise enemy is better than a foolish friend.

enemy : عدوّ - wise : عاقل - better : أفضل ، خَيْر - friend : صَديق - foolish : أحْمَق ، جاهِل

ٓalٓaāmelo ssayyٓe yalumo ٓadawāteh. 33 . العامِلُ السَّيِّءُ يلومُ أدَواتِه .

33. A bad worker always blames his tools.

worker : عامل - bad : رَديء ، سَيّء - blame : يَلوم - tools : أدَوات

ٓaane lmarٓ lā tasٓal wa sal ٓaan qarineh. 34 . عَنِ المَرْءِ لا تَسْأَلْ وسَلْ عن قَرينهِ .

(sal=ٓesٓal)

34. A man is known by the company he keeps.

man : مَرْء ، رَجُل - company : قَرين ، رَفيق - keep : يَحْفظ ، يَبْقى مع

35 . عِنْدَ الإمْتِحانِ يُكْرَمُ المرْءُ أو يُهان .

(test : امتحان - be respected : يكرَم - be disrespected : يُهان).

ٓaenda lٓemteḥān yokramo lmarٓ ٓaw yohān.

35. The workman is known by his work.

ٓarrashwato taḥollo shāshata lqāḍi. 36 . الرَّشْوَةُ تَحُلُّ شاشَةَ القاضي .

36. No lock will hold against the power of gold.

bribe : رَشْوَه - untie : تَحُل - turban : شاشَه ، لَفّة - judge : قاضي

kollo mamnuٓa marghub. 37 . كُلُّ مَمْنوع مَرْغوب .

37. Forbidden fruit is sweetest.

forbidden: مَمْنوع - desired, wished for: مَرْغوب - sweetest: الأحْلى

38. كُلُّ إناء بما فيه يَنْضَح . kollo ẻnā›en bemā fihe yanḍaḥ.

38. A vessel filters what it contains.

vessel : وعاء، إناء – filters : يَرْشَح، يَنْضَح – contains : بما فيه، يَحتوي

This is said to comment about a person's bad words.

39. كَثْرَةُ الطَّبّاخين تُتْلِفُ الطَّبخه . kathrato ṯṯabbākhin totlefo ṯṯabkhah.

39. Too many cooks spoil the broth .

cooks : طبّاخين – spoil : تُتْلِف – broth : حَساء (soup)، طَبْخَه

40. الكَذِبُ حَبْلُهُ قَصير . ả̉l kadhebo ḥabloho qaṣir.

40. A liar should have a good memory.

lying : كَذِب – liar : كذّاب – rope : حَبْل – short : قَصير

The English words differ from the Arabic diction. The meaning is clear showing that the liar will be discovered sooner or later; there fore he should have a good memory!

41. كَثيرُ الكارات قَليلُ البارات . kathiro lkārāte qalilo lbārāt .

41. A rolling stone gathers no moss.

business: عَمَل، كار، صَنْعه - money :(colloquial : بارات)، نُقود

This is about a man who can do many kinds of work, but is not good at any one; and as a result he has little money.

42. الكَسَلُ رأسُ كُلِّ فَساد . ả̉lkasalo raả̉so kolle fasād.

42. Idleness is the source of all evil.

idleness : كَسَل – source : رأس، أصْل – evil : فَساد، شَرّ

**43**. لِكُلِّ جوادٍ كَبْوَه ،ولِكُلِّ عالِمٍ هَفْوَه .

lekolle jawāden kabwah, walekolle ʿāālemen hafwah.

43. Any horse may stumble, any sage may err.

horse: حِصَان، جَوَاد - Stumble: يَعْثُر، كَبْوَه - sage: حكيم (عالِم) - err: يُخْطِيء

هَفْوَه: خَطَأ – هَفَا: أخْطَأ

**44**. لِكُلِّ طَلْعَةٍ نَزْلَه – لِكُلِّ وَرْدَةٍ شَوْكَه .

lekolle ṭalʿaaten nazlah - lekolle wardaten shawkah.

44. Every medal has the reverse (medal:وِسام - reverse:مُضادّ، عكْسي)

ascent: طَلْعَه - descent: نَزْلَه - rose: وَرْدَه - thorn: شَوْكَه

The words of the English proverb are different from those of the Arabic proverb, but they give the same meaning.

There is no full and permanent advantage in a good thing, we have to expect some change or disadvantage. (medal and reverse - ascent and descent)

**45**. لا دُخانَ بدون نار .

lȁ dokhāna bedune nār.

45. No smoke without fire. (smoke : دُخان – without : بدون – fire : نار)

This is about a rumour which is not without origin.

**46** .لِكُلِّ مُشكِلةٍ حَلّ .

lekolle moshkelaten ḥall.

46. Every cloud has a silver lining.

cloud: سَحَابَه - (here means مُشْكِلَه) - solution: حَلّ

The Arabic diction is different from the English one. But in general, this means that after cloudy and stormy weather there will be rain. (silver lining)

lelhiṭān ʾadhān. 47. لِلحيْطان آذان .

47. Walls have ears

walls: جُدْران ، حِيطان - ears: آذان

This is said to warn a person who is speaking about something that may entail injury. It advises him to be cautious.

lā rāḥata duna taʿaab. 48. لا راحةَ دونَ تَعَبْ .

48. No pains, no gains.

pain: تَعَب ، ألَم - without: دون - gain: رِبْح ، راحَه

lā tuqeḍhe lfetnah. 49. لا توقِظِ الفِتْنَه .

49. Let sleeping dogs lie.

don't waken: لا توقِظ (let ... lie) - problem: مُشْكِله ، فِتْنَه

If you waken the sleeping dogs, they will bite you and by doing this you wakened the problem.

lā tajni mena shshawke lʿaenab. 50. لا تَجْني من الشَّوْكِ العِنَب .

50. You can't get blood out of a stone.

You can't make a purse out of a sow's ear.

get: تَحْصُل على ، تَجْني - blood: دَم - stone: حَجَر - out of: مِنْ - purse: جَزْدان

make: تَصْنع - sow: خَنْزيَرة - ear: أُذُن

You can't make (get) something good out of something bad.

lā yafello lḥadida ělla lḥadid. . لا يَفِلُّ الحديدَ إلاّ الحـديد .51

51. Diamond cut diamond.

iron: حَديد - cut: يَقْطع ، يَفِلّ - diamond: . ألْماس

lā taṭraḥ jawāherak ảmama lkhanāzir. . لاتَطْرَحْ جواهرِك أمامَ الخَنازير .52

52. Don't cast your pearls before swine.

cast: تُلْقي ، تطْرَح - pearls: جَواهِر - before: أمام - swine: خَنْزير

Don't offer a valuable thing before somebody who doesn't understand how valuable it is.

leḍḍarurate ảḥkām. . لِلضَّرورَةِ أحْكام .53

53. Necessity knows no law.

necessity: ضَرورَه - laws: قَوانين ، أحْكام

lā taqol ful qabla ản taḍaảa fi lảodul. . لاتَقُلْ فُول قَبْلَ أنْ تَضعَ في العُدول .54

54. Don't count your chickens before they are hatched.

bean: فول - put: تَضع - sacks: عُدول ، أكْياس - count: يَعُدّ - chickens: فراريج

hatch: يَفْقِس .

lā yaroddo lbokā lmayyet. . لا يرُدُّ البكاءُ المَيِّتْ .55

55. It's no use crying over spilt milk.

crying: البُكاء - dead: الميّت - no use: لا فائِدَة - spilt: مُراق - milk: حليب

The lost thing is lost. Don't waste your time bemoaning it.

56 .الدَّهْرُيَوْمان :يَوْمٌ لَكَ ويومٌ عَلَيْكَ . .(عَليك :on you – لَك :for you – زَمان ، دَهْر :time)

ảddahro yawmān: yawmon laka wa yawmon ẚalayk

56. Every dog has his day.

57 .ما تَجْلِبُه الرِّياحُ تَأْخذُهُ الزَّوابِعِ . mā tajleboho rreyāḥo tảkhodhoho zzawābeẚ..

57. Easy come, easy go.

bring : تَجْلِب ، تُحضِر – winds : رياح – take : يَأْخُذ – storms : زَوَابِع

what is got easily without effort, (got by the wind)

will be soon taken away (taken by the storms).

58 .مَصائِبُ قَوْمٍ عِنْدَ قَوْمٍ فَوائِدُ . maṣāẻbo qawmen aẻnda qawmen fawāẻdo.

58. One man's meat is another man's poison.

Misfortunes of some people are advantages to others.

advantages : فَوائِد ، مَنافِع – meat : لَحْم – poison : سُمّ – misfortunes : مَصائب ، سُوء حَظّ

59 .مَنْ حَسُنَتْ سِياسَتُهْ دامَتْ رِياسَتُهْ . man ḥasonat seyāsatoh dāmat reyāsatoh.

59. He who governs well may last long.

govern: يحكم ، يسوس - last: يَدُوم - may: مُمْكِن - principal ship: رياسَه

60 .مَنْ كَثُرَ ضَحِكُه قَلَّتْ هَيْبَتُه . man kathora ḍaḥekoh qallat haybatoh.

60. As laughter increases, respect decreases.

laughter: ضَحِك - increase: يكثُر ، يَزْداد - decrease: يَقِلّ - respect: هَيْبَه ، إحترام

61 .مِفْتاحُ الشَّرِ كَلِمَهْ. meftāḥo shsharre kalemah.

61. The key to evil is one word.

key: مفتاح - evil: شرّ - one word: كَلمه

62 .اَلْوَلَدُ سِرُّ أَبيه . ảl walado serro ảbih.

62. A chip of (off) the old block.

The words of the English. proverb are totally different from the Arabic diction. The meaning is that the boy is like his father.

boy: وَلَد - secret: سرّ - (here it means like مِثْل) - his father: أبيه - chip: قِطْعه

block: كَتْلَه خَشَبيَّه أو حَجَريّه

63 .مَنْ بَعْدِ نَفْسِكْ إِنْفَع صَديقَك . men baẩde nafsek ẻnfaẩ ṣadiqak.

63. Charity begins at home.

charity: عَمل خَيْر ، إحسْان - yourself: نَفْسك - help: إنْفَع ، سَاعِد - friend: صَديق

The saying is said by a man who is expected to help others, he says that after helping my family I will help others.

or: to a person who takes care of others without taking care of his family.

64 .مُستَرْخِصُ اللَّحْمِ يَنْدَمُ عِنْدَ المَرَقه .

mostarkheṣo llaḥme yandamo ẩenda lmaraqah.

64. Good cheap is dear.

cheap: رَخيص - dear: عَزيز ، غال - Person looking for cheap things: مُسْتَرْخِص

meat: لَحْم - regrets: يَأسَف ، يَنْدَم - broth, thin soup: مَرَقه

The person who buys cheap meat, for example, will regret when he finds the soup of this meat is distasteful. This is true for any other

cleanliness: نَظَافه - next to: بَعْدَ - godliness: تُقىً، صَلاح ، إيمان

cheap things. Therefore good and cheap material is dear.

65 .مَنْ يَتوكّلْ على الله ما خابَ رَجاه .«إعْقلْ وتوكّل» .

man yatawakkal ʿaala llāh mā khaba rajāh.

65. He who serves God has a good master.

serve God: trust in God, depend on ....: يتوكّل علىَ - failed: فَشلَ، خابَ

hope: أمَل رَجاء - his hope: رَجاؤه، رجاه

Who trusts in God, after doing his best, will not fail.

- Do your best: إعقِل, and trust in God: توكّل على الله

ʾal mālo lḥarāmo lā yadum. 66 .المالُ الحَرامُ لا يَدوم .

66. Illgotten wealth is not lasting.

Wealth: ثَرْوَه، مال - illgotten: حَرام - doesn't last: لا يَدوم

man hāba khāb. 67 .مَنْ هابَ خاب .

67. Nothing venture, nothing gain.

Who: مَنْ - was afraid, didn't venture: هابَ - failed: فَشلَ، خابَ

gained nothing: فَشِلَ، خابَ - gain: يَحْصَل على، يكْسَب - nothing: لا شَيْء

mā ḥakka jeldak methlo ḍhofrek. 68 .ما حَكَّ جِلْدَك مِثْلُ ظُفْرِك .

68. The master's eye makes the horse fat.

Scratch: يَحُكّ - skin: جِلْد - like: مِثْل - nail: ظُفر

Here, the English words of the proverb differ from the Arabic ones.

The meaning is the same. If you don't depend on others to do your affairs, you will succeed, just the same case with the owner of a horse who will take care of his horse by himself, his horse will be fat.

ảl maldugho yakhāfo men jarrate lḥabl. . **69 .المَلْدوغُ يَخافُ مِنْ جَرَّةِ الحَبْل**

69. A burnt child dreads the fire.

bitten: مَلْدوغ - dread, fear: يخاف - coil, rope: حَبْل - movement: حَرَكه، جرّه

The bitten child by a snake will be afraid of the movement of a rope thinking it to be a snake. The same case with the burnt child will be aware of the fire and will avoid it.

man ṭalaba lảolā sahera llayāli. . **70 .مَن طَلَبَ العُلى سَهِرَ اللّيالي**

70. He who deserves top, must sit up many nights.

deserve: يَسْتَحِقّ، يَطْلب - top, eminence: عُلى - sit up: يَسْهر - nights: لَيالي

**71 .ما كُلُّ ما يَتمنّى المَرْءُ يُدْرِكُهُ تَجْري الرِّياحُ بِما لا تَشْتَهي السُّفُنُ .**

mā kollo mā yatamanna lmar› yodrekoho

tajri rreyāḥo bemā lā tashtahi ssofono.

71. A man doesn't attain all his heart's desires,

for the wind doesn't blow as the vessels wish.

attain: يَحصُل على، يُدرِك - desires: يرْغب، يتَمنّى - blow: تَهُبّ، تَجْري

wind: ريح - vessels: مَراكِب، سُفُن - wish: تَرْغب - all: كُلّ

mā kollo mā yalmaảo dhahaban. **72 .ما كُلُّ ما يَلْمَعُ ذَهَبا .**

ما كُلُّ سَوْداءَ فَحْمَه ولا كلُّ حَمْراءَ لَحْمة .

mā kollo sawdāɔ faḥmah, walā kollo ḥamrāɔ lahmah

72. All that glitters is not gold.

glitter: يَلْمَع - gold: ذَهَب - black: سَوْداء - coal: فَحْمه - red: حَمْراء - meat: لَحْمَه

73. ما تَزْرَعْ تَحْصُدْ . mā tazraå taḥṣod.

73. As you sow, you shall reap (mow).

sow: تَبْذُر، تزرع - reap: تَحْصُد - now: تَحْصُد

74. مَنْ طَلَبَ الكَثيرَ خَسِرَ القليل . man ṭalaba lkathir khasera lqalil.

74. grasp all, lose all.

grasp: يُمسِك، يطلب - all: كُلّ، كثير - lose: يَخْسر

If you have got a little of something, don't refuse this hoping to get more, because you will lose this little and by this you will lose all. Don't be too greedy.

75. نَحْنُ في التَّفكْير واللّه في التَّدْبير . naḥno fi ttafkir wallaho fi ttadbir.

75. Man proposes, God disposes.

propose: يَقْتَرِح، يفكّر - dispose: يُقَرِّر، يُدَبِّر

76. النَّظافةُ مِنَ الإيمان . ȃnnaḍhāfato mena lȇimān.

76. Cleanliness is next to godliness.

cleanliness : نظافه – next to = بَعد – goodliness = ايمان – تقى

77. نِعْمَ المؤَدِّبُ العصا . neåma lmoȃddebo låaṣā.

77. Spare the rod, spoil the child.

spare: لا تَسْتَعمل، يُوَفِّر - rod: عَصا - spoil: يُفْسِد، يُتْلِف - child: طِفْل

If you don't use the rod - a symbol of punishment - you will spoil the child.

therefore discipline - rod - is the best tuitor: مُؤَدِّب

**78** . الوَحْـدَةُ خَيْرٌ مِنْ جَلِيسِ السُّوء . ảl waḥdato khayron men jalise ssu›.

78. Better be alone than in bad company .

alone: وَحيد - better: أفْضل مِن ، خَيْر - company: جَليس ، رفيق - bad: سَيِّء

**79** . النَّعْجةُ الـجَرْباءُ تُعْدي القَطيع . ảnnaảjato ljarbā› toảdi lqatiả.

79. Ill weed mars a whole pot of pottage.

Sheep: نَعْجة - scabby: جَرْباء - infect: يُعْدي - flock: قَطِيع - ill: سَيِّء ، رَديء

weed: عُشْبَه ضارَّة - mar: يُفسِد - pottage: حِساء (soup)

The English words of the proverb differ from the Arabic ones.

The meaning is clear: one bad element will spoil a lot of good elements if associated with them.

**80** . نَبْحُ الكِلابْ لا يَضُرُّ السَّحابْ . nabḥo lkelāb lā yaḍorro ssaḥāb.

80. To bark the moon.

bark: يَنْبَح ، نَبْح - dogs: كلاب - doesn't harm: لا يَضُرّ - clouds: سحاب - moon: قَمَر

The English words of the proverb are different from the Arabic ones, but the meaning is the same.

The barking of the dogs does not affect the moon.

The barking, the attack on a ligh person, does not affect him, as the barking on the moon doesn't either.

**81** . يَدٌ وَحْدَها لا تُصفِّق . yadon waḥdahā lā toṣaffeq.

81. One flower makes no garland.

hand: يَد - alone: وَحْدها - clap: تُصَفِّق - doesn't clap: لا تُصَفِّق - flower: زَهْر

garland: إِكْليل زَهْر

Here also, the English words of the proverb are different from the Arabic ones. The meaning in both proverbs is clear.

ʾeʿaqel wa tawakkal. **82** . إعْقِلْ وتَوكَّلْ .

82. God helps those who help themselves.

think: إعْقِل ، فكِّر - plan: خَطِّطْ - trust in God: تَوكَّل - God: اللّه - help: يُساعِد

those: أُولئِك - themselves: أَنْفُسَهُم

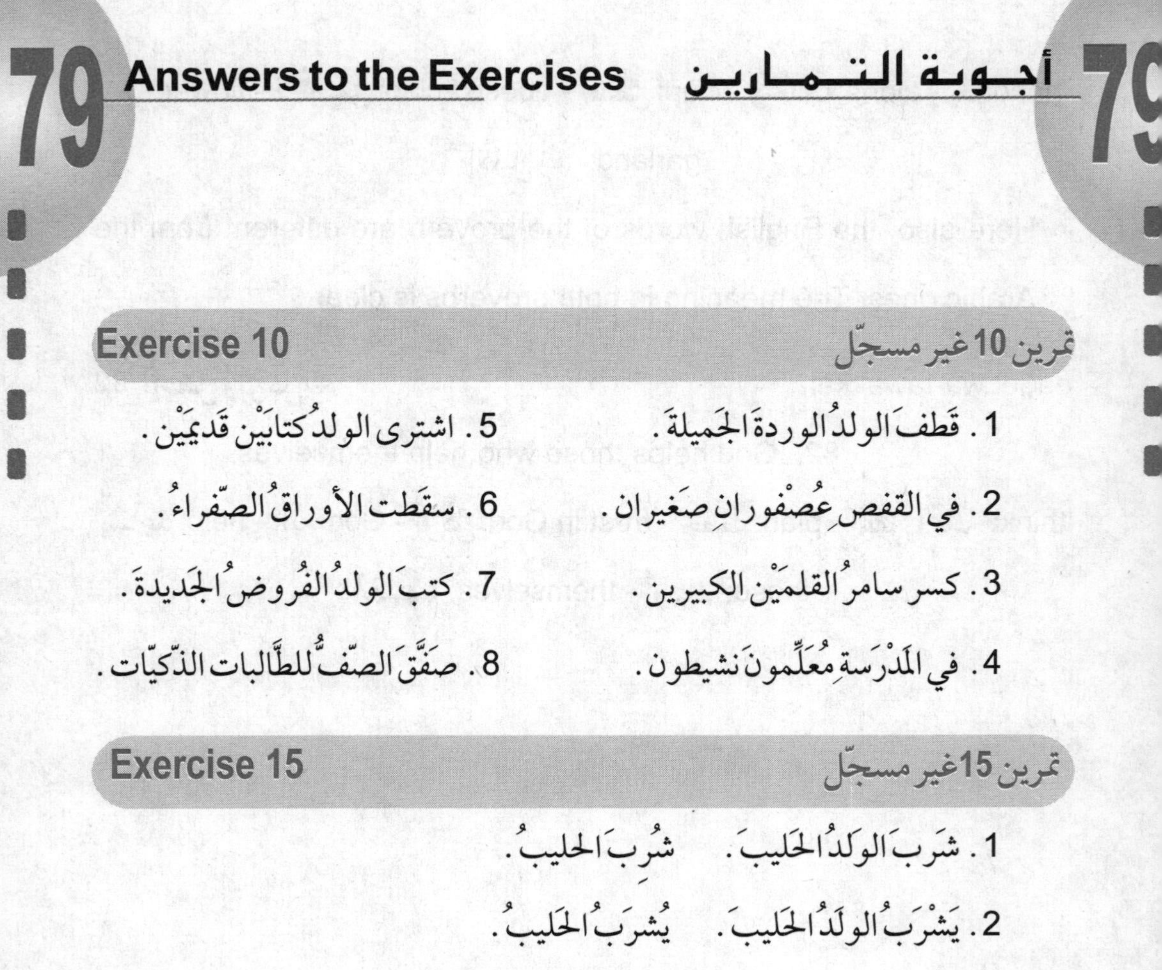

## Exercise 10 تمرين 10 غير مسجّل

1. قَطفَ الولدُ الوردةَ الجَميلةَ .
2. في القفصِ عُصفورانِ صَغيران .
3. كسر سامرُ القلمَيْن الكبيرين .
4. في المَدْرَسةِ مُعلّمونَ نشيطون .
5. اشترى الولدُ كتابَيْن قَديمَيْن .
6. سقَطت الأوراقُ الصّفراءُ .
7. كتبَ الولدُ الفُروضُ الجَديدةَ .
8. صَفّقَ الصّفُّ للطّالبات الذّكيّات .

## Exercise 15 تمرين 15 غير مسجّل

1. شَربَ الولدُ الحَليبَ . شُرِبَ الحليبُ .
2. يَشرْبُ الولَدُ الحَليبَ . يُشرَبُ الحَليبُ .
3. سَمعَ المعلّمُ الصَّوتَ . سُمِعَ الصَّوتُ .
4. يَسْمَعُ المُعَلمُ الصَّوتَ . يُسْمَعُ الصَّوتُ .

## Exercise 17 تمرين 17 غير مسجّل

1. أرادَ الأولادُ أن يشربوا .
2. خَرجوا كي يَلْعبوا .
3. دَرسا كي يَنْجَحا .
4. لم يكتُبوا فرُوضَهم .

5. لماذا لم تأخُذي الدَّواءَ؟

6. الصَّيادونَ يَصيدونَ السَّمكَ.

7. العاملانِ يَعْملانِ في الحقلِ.

8. أنتِ تُنظفّين الغُرْفةَ كُلَّ يوم.

## Exercise 19 تمرين 19 غير مسجّل

1. يَصيدُ الصّيادونَ الطيورَ

2. ساعدْتُ المُحْتاجينَ.

3. جاءَ أخوهُ مِنَ الخارِج.

4. زُرْنا أخاهُ المَريضَ.

5. قَرأَ أحْمَدُ قِصّتَيْن.

6. السَّمكُ في البَحْرِ.

7. الكِتابُ أفْضَلُ صَديق.

8. أهْدَيْنا المُعلماتِ هَديّةً.

9. جاءَ الصّديقُ باسِمًا.

10. أُحِبُّ الفاكِهَةَ طازَجةً.

## Exercise 21 تمرين 21 غير مسجّل

1. هَذا الكِتابُ مُفيدٌ.

2. هَذِهِ الزّهرةُ جَميلةٌ .

3. ذلكَ الوَلَدُ يَلْعَبُ في الحقلِ .

4. تِلكَ البِنْتُ تَلْعَبُ بالكرةِ .

5. هَؤُلاءِ الأَوْلادُ يَلْعبون .

6. أَعْطى المُعلِّمُ هاتَيْنِ البنتَيْنِ جائِزَتَيْن .

7. عَطفْتُ على هذيْنِ الفقيرَيْنَ .

8. هَؤُلاءِ البنات يَجتهِدْنَ في دُروسِهِنَّ .

9. هَذانِ المَلْعبانِ واسعان .

## Exercise 23 — تمرين 23 غير مسجّل

1. الطَّبيعةُ جَميلةٌ . أصبحَتِ الطَّبيعةُ جَميلةً .

2. الدَّرْسُ سَهلٌ . لَيْسَ الدرسُ سَهْلاً .

3. الوَلَدُ خائِفٌ . كانَ الولدُ خائفًا .

4. الرَّجُلُ غَنِيٌّ . صار الرجلُ غَنيًا .

## Exercise 24 — تمرين 24 غير مسجّل

1. الطَّقْسُ جَميلٌ . إنَّ الطَّقْسَ جَميلٌ .

2. الدَّواءُ نافعٌ . لعلَّ الدّواءَ نافعٌ .

3. الزَّهْرُ إكْليلٌ . كَأنَ الزَّهْرَ إكْليلٌ .

4. البَحْرُ هادِىءٌ.  لَيْتَ البَحرَ هادِىءٌ.

5. الغائِبُ قادِمٌ.  إنَّما الغائبُ قادمٌ.

## Exercise 26  تمرين 26 غير مسجّل

| | صاحب الحال | الحال |
|---|---|---|
| 1. رَجَعَ أخوكَ مِنَ الرِّحْلَةِ ناجحًا. | أخوك | ناجحًا |
| 2. لا تشرَبِ الماءَ كَدِرًا. | الماءَ | كَدِرًا |
| 3. جاء زَيدٌ راكِبًا. | زَيدٌ | راكِبًا |
| 4. شاهَدْتُ العامِلَ يَزْرَعُ الحَقْلَ. | العامِلَ | يزرعُ الحقلَ (جملة) |
| 5. رأيتُ العُصفورَ على الشَّجَرةِ. | العُصْفورَ | على الشجرةِ (شبه جملة) |
| 6. شاهَدْتُ الطِّفلَ وهو يبكي. | الطِّفلَ | وهوَ يبكي (جملة) |

## Exercise 29  تمرين 29 غير مسجّل

1. المرأةُ التي تَهُزُّ السَّريرَ بيمينِها تَهُزُّ العالَمَ بِيَسارِها.

2. ما تَزْرَعْ تَحْصُدْ.

3. هَؤُلاءِ هُمُ الَّذينَ فازوا.

4. صَديقُكَ هُوَ الَّذي يُخلِصُ لَكَ.

5. مَنْ يَجتَهِدْ يَنْجَحْ.

6. عاقَبَتِ المُعَلِّمةُ الطَّالباتِ اللَّواتي أهمَلْنَ واجبَهُنَّ.

7. هذانِ هما الصَّديقانِ اللَّذان زارانا.

8. عرَفْتُ البنتَيْنِ اللَّتَيْنِ نالتا الجائِزةَ.

## تمرين 32 غير مسجّل — Exercise 32

1. اشترَتِ البِنْتُ خاتِمَيْ ذَهَب.

2. ألْقى أُسْتاذُ العُلومِ مُحاضَرةً.

3. زارَ عُضْوا البَرْلَمانِ رَوْضةَ الأطْفالِ.

4. أصبَحَتْ شَوارِعُ القَرْيَةِ نَظيفَةً.

5. كُنْ أميناً لِأنَّ الأَمانةَ أَفْضَلُ سِياسةٍ.

## تمرين 35 غير مسجّل — Exercise 35

1. زارني جَميعُ المَدْعوّين إلاّ واحداً.

2. لَمْ يَنْجَحْ غَيْرُ عليٍّ.

3. لَمْ يَأكُلْ سَعيدٌ إلاّ تُفَّاحَتَيْن.

4. لَمْ يَفْشَلْ في الإمْتِحانِ إلاّ إثْنان.

5. ما جاء القَوْمُ إلاّ سليمٌ. (هنا يجوز النصب كذلك: إلاّ سليماً)

6. سَمِعَ الجميعُ النِّداءَ غيرَ واحدٍ.

## Exercise 37 تمرين 37 غير مسجّل

1. اشترى الولدُ تِسْعةَ كُتُبٍ .

2. باعَ الرَّجُلُ أَرْبعَ مَحْفَظاتٍ .

3. تخرّجَ من كُلِّيَّةِ الحُقوقِ خَمْسَ عَشْرةَ فتاةً وستَّةَ عَشَرَ شابًا .

4. يوجَدُ في المَدْرَسةِ عَشْرةُ صُفُوف . في الصّفِّ الأوَّلِ خمسةٌ وعِشرونَ وَلَداً .

وفي الصَّفِّ الثاني إحْدى وعِشْرون بنْتًا .

5. في مكْتَبتي ألْفُ كِتابٍ ومائةُ مَجلَّةٍ .

6. أكلَ الرَّجُلُ بَيْضتَيْن اثْنَتيْنِ ورَغيفًا واحداً .

## Exercise 40 تمرين 40 غير مسجّل

1. قرأتُ الدَّرسَ الثالثَ عشرَ .

2. كَتَبْتُ الصَّفْحَةَ الحادِيَةَ والخَمْسين .

3. قرأتُ المَقالَةَ الثّامِنةَ .

4. أنا في العامِ الرَّابعَ عشرَ مِنْ عُمْري .

5. أُخْتي في السَّنةِ العِشْرينَ منْ عمْرها .

6. أخي في العامِ الخامِسِ والأرْبعينَ من عُمْرِهِ .

7. ألصَّفْحَةُ المائةُ .

8. ألْعامُ الألْفُ .

## Exercise 41 تمرين 41 غير مسجّل

1. إنَّها السّاعَةُ الخامِسَةُ .

2. إنّها السَّاعَةُ السَّابِعةُ والنِصّفْ .

3. إنّها العاشِرَةُ إلاّ خَمْسَ دَقائق .

4. تُصْبِحونَ عَلى خَيْر .

5. إنَّها السَّادِسةُ والرُّبْع .

6. مَساءُ الخَيْر .

7. صَباحُ الخيْر .

# CONTENTS

# الفهرست